Effective Program Evaluation

The Nelson-Hall Series in Sociology

Consulting Editor: Jonathan H. Turner
University of California, Riverside

Effective Program Evaluation

An Introduction

Daniel Krause
Roosevelt University

Nelson-Hall Publishers / Chicago

Project Editor: Dorothy Anderson
Cover Painting: *Event Horizon* by Heidi Hybl

Library of Congress Cataloging-in-Publication Data

Krause, Daniel Robert.
    Effective program evaluation : an introduction / Daniel Krause.
       p.   cm.
    Includes index.
    ISBN 0-8304-1390-1
    1. Evaluation research (Social action programs) I. Title.
H62.K683   1995
361'.0068'4 – dc20   95-14908
                                                          CIP

Manufactured in the United States of America

10   9   8   7   6   5   4   3   2

The paper used in this book meets the
minimum requirements of American
National Standard for Information
Sciences—Permanence of Paper for
Printed Library Materials, ANSI
Z39.48-1984.

To Old Friends

Contents

Preface

I wrote this book primarily for individuals not previously involved in program evaluations. This audience includes graduate and undergraduate students taking their first course in Program Evaluation, and it includes program managers, people who should know more about a process that is an integral part of their individual and organizational well-being. The potential audience might also include administrators in both government and private agencies who are trying to allocate their funds reasonably and effectively.

It was confusing sometimes to determine who might need what and how much of it they needed. Whenever there was a potential conflict, I went in the direction of the greatest simplicity. It was frustrating because there was no way to be sure that those decisions were correct. The final assessment will be made by the people who read the book.

I did not plan this book as a comprehensive and detailed examination of every procedure and issue in program evaluations. Interested readers can find such discussions in other texts. Those discussions are, necessarily perhaps, long, involved, and tedious. But these books often turn readers off before they have the chance to appreciate the unique challenges and special enjoyment that comes from a well-executed program evaluation.

What I want to accomplish here is what years of teaching courses in Program Evaluation have convinced me was needed — a book that gives readers a good working introduction to the evaluation process. You can expect this book to help you achieve that understanding. But it will not suffice as the sole source of material for this frequently complex process. Both students and instructors should regard this book as an initial, or perhaps supplemental, resource.

With reasonable attention to the material, readers can expect the following results:

1. They should *get a working understanding* of the principles in program evaluation.
2. They will acquire an *appreciation of the complexity of the issues involved.* Part of this appreciation includes recognizing the alternative approaches to dealing with various issues.
3. They will develop some *ability to design an effective program evaluation* and/or to assess the evaluations done by others.

These three goals were enough for one text. Even these more limited intentions were possible only because I elected to keep many explanations and discussions uncomplicated. It is not that the explanations in the book are overly simple; my primary intention is to provide readers with a working understanding of the evaluation process, and understanding evaluation research is easier when the individual learns the basic principles first. It makes no sense to discuss complicated processes before the basics are understood. A concentration on basics is as important in evaluation research as it is in mastering a sports activity. If the fundamentals are mastered, the student can apply them even in situations that are different or more complex.

Technical procedures are discussed here but generally not in detail. Items such as questionnaire construction and statistical analysis, for example, are important components in many program evaluations. But to discuss the particulars of these procedures would require far more time and space than I thought reasonable.

This focus on general topics has not resulted in the omission of essential points or issues. I discuss, for example, the use of a questionnaire in the evaluation process. I review the value that this data-gathering technique has for program evaluations and the procedure's special strengths and weaknesses. As far as the questionnaire is concerned, the reader will get an understanding of what this data-gathering process is all about and when it might be of value to the evaluation process. Those who want to get more detail on aspects such as how to construct a questionnaire or how to design a "social desirability scale" can find that information elsewhere.

To provide some help with these searches, most of the chapters have suggested readings on the key topics covered in that chapter. These suggested readings were not selected at random, and they do not represent a comprehensive listing of the relevant literature. They are my personal preferences or, in some cases, suggestions from my colleagues. These suggested readings are guides, not injunctions.

Readability was a central guide throughout the writing process. In my research classes over the past fifteen years, I have heard one lament more than any other: "I'm not learning anything from the book." I suspect that many other instructors have heard similar complaints.

There is considerable substance to these student protests. Social science research texts often have what *Time* magazine once described as high "fog counts." Even the most dedicated students sometimes have trouble extracting a working grasp of the material because of the way it is presented. Research texts were almost impossible to read when I was a student, and they have not seemed to improve much since I moved to the front of the classroom. Writing a "readable" research text was almost a personal crusade.

One other decision I made involved footnotes. I ignored the traditional, and admittedly important, academic emphasis on footnotes. But the omission was intentional and not due to sloppy scholarship. In the interests of increasing the readability of this book, I made an effort to avoid statements or quotations that required footnoting. In other situations, I chose not to list the studies or other sources that would have provided support for whatever claims or assertions I made.

Mr. Robert Dennler, agent, made the publication of this book possible. He put me in touch with the editors at Nelson-Hall, people who were a pleasure to deal with from the start of the process. They did an outstanding job filing down the manuscript's rough edges. I also want to thank the reviewers who patiently read an early draft of the book. Mr. William Rose went through every chapter and made many helpful comments. Steve Balkin offered his insight and contributions to the chapter dealing with cost-benefit analysis. Rich Feinberg from SUNY–Stony Brook provided bibliographic assistance. And my wife, Mery, read the book with the critical eye of an elementary school teacher.

I wrote this book in the hope it would be a readable and informative overview of program evaluation and a helpful tool for those who have not had much experience with this process. I hope it works!

INTRODUCTION

A Quick Look at Evaluation Research

Imagine that you are a researcher who is asked to examine the results of a community program that provides job training to its unemployed citizens. How hard could a project like that be? Everything and everyone involved with the program are doing what they are supposed to do; training sessions occur every day, unemployed people look at the posted job listings, the people show up for job interviews, and according to the program personnel, the whole process works perfectly. Besides all that, everyone involved has stayed within their financial budgets. How could it get any better than that?

Unfortunately, quick descriptions like "working perfectly," or even the magic words "under budget" seldom satisfy the concerns of funding agencies. Most organizations distributing money these days, whether they are government agencies or private foundations, are interested in specifics about what a social program is doing. Generalities or personal impressions are rarely enough to convince anyone that a program is working the way it was intended, planned, or budgeted.

In the case of that community job program, a funding agency would probably ask how many people the program has trained and at how much time and what cost per individual. In addition, they would probably want to know what information the training sessions covered and how that material related to the specific needs of potential employers. They might also wonder if most of the trainees actually completed the program, whether they got good jobs at reasonable salaries, if they stayed in those positions, and if the employers were satisfied with the quality of the individuals who went through the training.

Program directors in agencies across the country are scrambling to justify their activities and to prove, to the extent they can, that their programs are having positive effects and that those efforts are worth the monies being spent.

Individuals who have had no program evaluation experience are often frustrated when they discover the amount of time needed to deal with even "simple" questions about what appear to be relatively uncomplicated programs. Although it seems that a program evaluation should be simpler than "regular" research, it seldom is. Acquiring an understanding of what any social program is doing, or what it is not doing and why, usually requires more than answering a few questions. Even if an evaluator has years of experience and the organization involved provides adequate time and sufficient resources for the evaluation (those are, not incidentally, some very significant "if's!"), few evaluations end up being as simple as everyone wants or expects.

Program evaluation is not simple, but neither is it impossible. A good way to visualize the process is to see it somewhere between those points, an area that includes some of both the simple and the impossible. How do evaluators generate the information they need to assess a social program? What kind of data are they looking for, and what data-gathering technique is the best one to use? How will the evaluators use the information to test whether the program is accomplishing anything?

Though there are always some problems with any program evaluation, the underlying source for many of the difficulties lies with the human element in those equations. When human beings are involved, nothing is simple! If researchers keep that fundamental point in the back of their minds, that realization will help to minimize the eventual, and inevitable, frustrations.

There is a lot we do not know about human behavior. And our inability to predict exactly what people are going to do in any given situation (or even close to it) makes program evaluations even more difficult. Many researchers forget this critical assumption about the unpredictability of human behavior when they start analyzing the data.

It is a good idea to remind everyone involved in the evaluation process, early and often, that those deceptively precise computerized tables and charts represent human behavior and not gear ratios—that sensitivity can help to moderate generalizations that are too broad and sweeping.

A community job training program is a good way to illustrate how various human factors can distort program effects. In this program, as noted earlier, evaluators are interested in whether the training sessions are providing unemployed people with entries into the job market. The central evaluation question seems fairly clear: Are the program participants getting jobs? Central perhaps, but the question is not easy to answer because of the human element!

The most important task at the beginning of any evaluation is to isolate what the program is doing that is *the cause,* or at least *a cause,* of the item in question, in this case, people getting jobs. Here, even if the program participants are getting new jobs, no reasonable evaluator will conclude that this fact alone means that the program is a success. It is possible that the program is performing well, but it is too early to jump to that conclusion. Skepticism is a trait that develops in individuals who do evaluation research.

A closer look at the situation involves asking whether the enrollment of unemployed individuals in the job training program is a *direct cause* of their eventual success in the job market. Is it possible that factors other than the formal job training explain the success the trainees are having in finding jobs?

The evaluators might discover, for example, that all of the people who attended training sessions were volunteers. People came to the training sites on their own, maybe in response to an ad in the newspaper or a notice posted on a bulletin board. This willingness is potentially an important characteristic. No one made these individuals come to training sessions. They registered for the classes on their own and did all the assigned work. Those actions show the existence of certain personality traits. The people who attended are different from those individuals who sit at home and wait for work opportunities to come to them.

These trainees are more motivated than some and perhaps most of their peers. If they are ambitious enough to register and then attend training sessions, it is reasonable to suppose that they might have found jobs whether or not they enrolled in the training program. These trainees would certainly have done better in the job market than their not-as-motivated associates even without the benefit of that program. It is possible, then, that the training program is taking credit for something that would have happened without it. This possibility is one that evaluators have to consider.

Looking at the human element in the evaluation equation also means looking at the potential influence of the "informal" interactions taking place during the training sessions. Individuals enrolled in those sessions did more than sit in their seats and listen to the instructor. They met other students before and after classes. They may have had coffee or lunch together and talked about everything from the class content to the latest election. Some of the people doubtlessly became friends.

The results of all these interactions are potentially important to the evaluators because of the effects those contacts could have on what the program is doing. Those "unplanned" interactions could strengthen the program's work, or they could hamper it. It is possible, for example, that some trainees got together in study groups and that these informal support groups made a big difference in how those people responded to the classroom material.

A few of the trainees may have formed their own networks to help each other with job searches. Such informal contacts could have produced some, or even most, of the jobs those individuals eventually obtained. Although informal networks were arguably a part of the "program," the effects of those networks are an *indirect* rather than a direct result of the program's efforts. The evaluators have to be careful to make that distinction.

It is also possible that a competitive attitude emerged from those training classes. Rather than help one another, the trainees may have tried to sabotage other members of the class to improve their own chances of finding a job. Evaluators have to be sensitive to the existence of such possibilities, however indirect, so that they can assess their influence on the "formal" program activities.

It would also be important to see what happened to individuals who left the training program before graduating. Was it the difficulty of the classroom material, the rigid structure and timing of the classes, or perhaps the personality of the trainer that prompted these early departures? Whatever the causes, the characteristics and motivations of these "dropouts" are a potentially important element in the evaluation of the program. It is possible that this job training program is causing more problems for some unemployed individuals than it is solving.

The evaluation process also has to look at the employers—the organizations hiring the graduates from the training program. Did these organizations have positive experiences with the trainees in both the long and the short term? Did some employers have better experiences than others, perhaps because of the types of jobs offered to the graduates? Was there any indication that the employees of those organizations had negative feelings about people who came from "some special government program"?

The human element in the evaluation often ends up complicating what started out as a simple question about a social program. An evaluation that begins with a deceptively easy task can expand into a comprehensive project that pulls the evaluators into complex areas of inquiry. After an evaluation begins, it is not unusual for the research efforts to scatter in different directions. Many of these efforts may be only remotely related to where the evaluators intended to go. Though this inquiry process can be positive, it can also easily get out of hand, unless the evaluators have the training to distinguish important questions from the nonessential ones.

Every individual in the process, from the research staff to the program manager, should agree at the outset that the purpose of the evaluation is to document what the program is doing. Although this statement seems obvious, it is an injunction that is surprisingly easy to forget, especially when the data begin to accumulate. The scattering of research efforts is not necessarily the result of inexperience or even poor planning. It is often the result of that frustrating human element that has a way of complicating even the most simple analysis.

Evaluators may have discovered early in their analysis of the job training program, for example, that trainees of one religious group were more inclined to enroll in the auto-repair job training sessions. Those of another group seemed particularly interested in office work, especially if computers were involved. Researchers would be understandably curious about those patterns. What facet of religion could explain these interesting results?

It is possible that the strength of individual religiosity determined those different career choices. If it were possible to examine what made some trainees more religious, it might be possible to explain career choice based on religious background. And, since the evaluators are on the topic, why not look at each person's family religious history? And so on.

When lines of analysis like these emerge, it is easy to understand how an evaluation of a community job program can quickly spin into uncharted and complex areas of inquiry. Although questions about topics such as religiosity can be interesting, they are usually not significant in the context of a program evaluation. Unless evaluators are equipped for a several year research commitment, they must be prepared to first distinguish the essential questions in the evaluation and then, appealing though they may be, brush the other questions to the side.

One other cornerstone for the construction of an effective program evaluation is the recognition that social programs, however comprehensive they may be, are only one element in the social lives of the people involved. Social programs are important activities, and the more comprehensive ones can significantly affect the lives of many people in addition to the actual participants. When a social program spends millions of dollars and employs hundreds of people, some significant results are inevitable.

But however large they are, these social programs are only one element in the fabric of people's lives. Evaluators as well as program managers need to remind themselves that people are involved in things other than program activities.

The individuals in a job program, for example, might be going to training sessions for eight hours every day of the work week. Although that schedule is a full-time commitment, there are still sixteen hours left in each day. The trainees go home after the classes to their families, friends, and communities. Lots of things can happen in those other sixteen hours to influence the attitudes and behavior of those people.

Those "other influences" affect the lives of the people who are in that job training program. What happens to those people and to their success or failure in the job market may have as much to do with these other factors as what took place within the training sessions. As difficult as it may be, evaluators have to recognize the potential role of the other factors and to incorporate this consideration into their analysis. This awareness is another reason for carefulness in any analysis.

At this early point, it is appropriate to point out and emphasize three fundamental principles (or limitations) that underlie the planning and design of effective program evaluations:

1. *A program evaluation involves human beings and human interactions.* This means that explanations will rarely be simple, and interpretations cannot often be conclusive.
2. *The primary purpose of a program evaluation is to isolate the effects of a given program's activities.* This means that evaluators should not extend their analysis in too many directions.
3. *A social program is only part of an individual's social life.* A program may have many effects, but it is not the only or seldom even the most important influence in an individual's life.

These three principles are not unique to program evaluations. In whole or in part, they would be found in most social science research activities. Evaluation research, then, is not unique in being hampered in its search for answers to questions about human behavior. Evaluation research is unique only in that it seeks to provide answers not to broad questions about that behavior but to more narrow queries about what is going on as a result of a particular set of program activities.

These three cornerstones are only the beginning of a long research process. Building on this initial framework means that the evaluators eventually have to consider a series of other questions, issues, and procedures. These other considerations are the material for the chapters in this book.

The practice of program evaluation is a complex activity, usually more complex and involved than people believe. Besides routine complexities, doing an effective evaluation also requires that the researchers be prepared to deal with an ongoing series of surprises. Those surprises and the ensuing complications can be difficult to deal with, but they make evaluation research particularly fascinating.

CHAPTER ONE

An Overview of Program Evaluation: Issues and Procedures

One way to begin developing a working understanding of program evaluation is to look at some general questions frequently asked about the procedure: What is program evaluation? What kind of preparation qualifies someone to do this type of research? And if there are so many problems with the process, why bother doing these studies? Some of these questions were touched on in the introductory section, but they all deserve a more thorough discussion.

First, what is a "program evaluation"? Program evaluation, or "evaluation research," refers to the research procedures and techniques used to examine the effectiveness of social programs. Program evaluation, in other words, is a process that generates the information used to describe what a program is doing and how well it does it.

The programs in question do not necessarily have to be "social" in nature (i.e., involving human beings). But since most programs of interest to evaluators involve human subjects, the examples used throughout this book will too. Readers who have interests in other, nonsocial types of programs, dog-training sessions, for example, do not have to feel left out of the discussions. Evaluations of programs involving nonhuman subjects will, to some extent, rely on many of the same procedures.

The definition of program evaluation also seems to exclude organizations in the private sector, but that exclusion is neither intentional nor absolute. Organizations in the public sector are just more likely to use formal evaluations. They need evaluations to provide information that will tell them how well, or how poorly, they are doing.

Private sector businesses have profit-and-loss statements. They find out how well they are doing, or how effective a particular segment of their business is, by looking at the bottom lines on their financial statements. If an activity or a certain product line shows a profit, it is doing well. If it doesn't, then it isn't. Most businesses are doing the equivalent of program evaluations constantly. So they rarely have a need for formal evaluations, at least the kind discussed here.

Still, it is possible that a business organization would be interested in doing an evaluation. A large corporation, for example, might decide to build and equip a comprehensive daycare center for workers' children. Although the company would (probably) not be interested in a "profit-loss" analysis of that center, they might be curious about whether the center was affecting their employees in a positive way, and not incidentally, how it was affecting the children.

In any case, the fact that the organization supplying the funding for a daycare program was General Dynamics rather than New York City would not change evaluation procedures. In cases involving the private sector, the basic principles of evaluation research would still apply.

These expansions on the initial definition of program evaluation suggest that the principles of evaluation research are applied in virtually every situation, even those not fitting the general outline of a "normal" evaluation situation. The various rules or principles may have to be slightly modified, but they are rarely discarded. Distinctive program settings, the character of the sponsoring organization, differences in the characteristics of the participants — these elements may alter how or to what extent the evaluator uses various techniques and procedures. But in program evaluations, the rules remain rules.

In evaluating any social program, the researchers have to get enough information to assess the effects of that program. Although evaluators are free to use whatever research technique is most appropriate, they usually get the necessary information from one or more of the data-gathering techniques most common in the social sciences.

Head Start is a fairly well-known, federally funded group of activities for preschoolers. The activities included in this program were designed to provide an educational "equalizer" for disadvantaged children. To obtain information about how this program is doing, evaluators would use some, perhaps even most, of the social science research techniques.

Formal interviews, for example, might be held with students and teachers to find out what they thought about the program. Questionnaires could be mailed to parents to find out the effects of the program on family households. It is also likely that researchers would sit in on some of the class sessions to watch and document what takes place. Finally, children's past and current school records might be reviewed to see whether the Head Start experience had a measurable effect on subsequent academic performance. All of this information is collected, analyzed, and interpreted in a way that will enable the appropriate individuals to judge whether the programs are doing what they were designed to do.

A few of the commonly used research techniques are not difficult to understand or to master. Some of them though, like observational techniques, require a degree of training and expertise. A few of the collection procedures, notably interviews, require considerable experience along with training before the researcher feels comfortable using them. Familiarity with data-gathering techniques is probably one of the most important skills an evaluator brings into the research process.

As important as they are, research skills are only one of the abilities that competent evaluators should have. After gathering information on the program, evaluators still must analyze and interpret those data in a reasonable, objective, and thorough fashion. There is a *substantial difference* between conducting a program evaluation and doing an *effective* one.

Several years ago, a Midwestern city agency was completing the third year of a federally funded grant on community crime prevention. The grant covered a variety of community-based activities, ranging from installing home privacy fences around apartment buildings to hiring security guards. The city had to arrange a formal evaluation as a condition for receiving federal funds, and they eventually hired a professional (accounting) firm for the task.

After about six months, the accounting firm issued an evaluation report for the city's Community Crime Prevention Program. Their report was lengthy and very professional in its appearance. The thick volumes contained hundreds of charts and tables. Unfortunately, the people at the housing agency had no idea what those volumes of data meant. Even the program director did not understand the implications of the figures and tables. More important, despite all the data, city officials could not provide specific evidence that the various community crime prevention activities were having a significant effect on the local crime rates. If the city people could not be certain about the program's effectiveness, how could they convince the federal government that it made sense to allocate more funds?

Despite good intentions, the evaluation conducted by that accounting firm produced a report that was fundamentally flawed. The biggest problem came from the fact that researchers approached the community crime program in the same way they dealt with an auditing situation. In crime analysis, it would be convenient if a homicide was exactly twice as serious as an armed robbery. Four armed

3

robberies, then, would be the same, analytically speaking, as two homicides. A homicide, in turn, might be equivalent to four assaults. If shoplifting was three times as bad as industrial water pollution, it would be reasonable to punish shoplifters with sanctions three times more severe than those given to polluters. Debit the crime account and credit the prison system; the social books would remain in balance. More important, the crime rates would be relatively easy to analyze!

But human behavior is not as precise as the accountants thought. Although numbers are used to categorize and describe human behavior, those numbers have to be examined with an awareness of what they represent and what they *do not* represent!

For example, Community A might have a homicide rate that is twice as high as that of Community B. But it would be foolish for researchers to conclude that the "problem" within Community A was twice as serious as the problem within Community B. Or that reactions to that violence within Community A would necessarily be twice as severe; or even that the residents in Community B would be only "half as worried" about violent crime as residents of Community A.

Numbers are seldom able to tell the whole story about the complexities and the dynamics of human behavior. Figures can be useful, but if the manipulation blinds researchers to seeing and understanding what those numbers represent, the analysis, and ultimately the evaluation, is going to be out of touch with reality. This could have been the problem with the evaluation done by the accounting firm.

In the last few years, program evaluation has established itself as an important player on the governmental policy stage. Data from program evaluations provide officials with information on individual social programs. Analyses also provide information that can help officials assess the underlying philosophies and policies that produced the programs. The policy implications of program evaluations sometimes turn out to be more important than the programmatic assessments.

Considering the implications of a program evaluation, it is not an overstatement to describe this research as an important process. It should not be unreasonable to suggest that the people who design these investigations should have the skills necessary to do those tasks properly. Though this conclusion might be obvious, deciding on the content of those "skills" may not be so easy.

Part of the uncertainty about what constitutes proper training for an evaluator stems from the frequent confusion of program evaluation with other types of social research. Research based on more scholarly pursuits is not necessarily more important nor is it inherently more precise than evaluation research. It is simply different.

4

The two do have some commonalities: they often use the same data-gathering techniques; they rely on many of the same measurement devices; and they often draw on the same body of scientific literature for clarification and support. Yet they are different in some important ways.

One critical difference is the goal of the research. In scholarly or what is sometimes described as "pure" research, social scientists start with hypotheses, gather their data, and then try to form generalizations about the results. In this interactive process of analysis and interpretation, social science researchers try to build on the theoretical frameworks of their disciplines. A search for theory is the primary function of their scholarly research, and this quest for theory and for theoretically significant relationships requires social scientists to use research procedures in a fashion that is often different from what generally occurs within program evaluations.

Correlation coefficients, for example, are a popular statistical means of testing for potential relationships between variables. But statistically significant correlations of variables that might produce a scientific journal article could easily be meaningless to an agency director who is trying to decide whether to spend another million dollars on a particular program. A statistically significant correlation, in other words, does not necessarily have practical value.

In the community crime prevention program mentioned earlier, a social scientist could spend months looking for every possible statistical relationship in the data: how does family size correlate with violence? Does individual educational level make a difference in the rate of automobile theft? Are females more likely to go to jail for shoplifting than males?

These and a hundred other questions are fodder for social science journal articles. But the time and effort devoted to these and other potentially important questions still may not address the central concerns of either managers or funding agencies. Considerable money was spent on a community crime prevention program, and the only important question for the people involved with that program is, Did the crime rate go down?

"Forget the theories and the complex statistics. Just tell us what happened." This statement is the type of instruction that evaluators frequently get. Their research directions, as a result, are often different from those taken by the more traditional social scientist.

Drawing a line between scholarly inquiries and evaluation research does not mean that the two types of research have to be separated as though they were angry spouses. Despite the fundamental difference in basic goals, evaluators can draw important insights from the scientific literature, and the reverse is equally true. If the goals of an evaluation are fully understood and the evaluator does not structure the evaluation to fit the requirements of a journal publication, the working relationships between the two types of research can and should be mutually beneficial.

Another distinction between the two types of research lies with the nature of the analysis that is done. A term often used in the scientific literature is "level of sophistication," a designation applied to various research projects. That term has some important connotations applicable to scholarly research but is often unreasonable if applied to evaluations.

The popular reasons for labeling a project "sophisticated" are usually the use of larger data sets, the application of more complex statistical analyses, or the use of the "more scientific" techniques. Research with a sample size of one thousand is presumably more sophisticated than one with a sample size of fifty. Similarly, a research study that uses complex statistical analysis is considered more sophisticated than an analysis that uses only simple percentages. And finally, a project that uses a questionnaire would likely be considered more sophisticated than one that relies on personal interviews.

If sophistication were used to mean the ability to impress an audience, then the term might be appropriate. It is not difficult to impress an audience by discussing large numbers or by using complex statistical formulae. The audience might not understand a correlation matrix, and the researcher could impress them with the fact that they did not understand it.

There is nothing wrong with large sample sizes or with complex statistics. And there is nothing wrong with using a questionnaire to gather information. By themselves, though, larger data sets, more complex statistical procedures, and the use of certain research techniques do not necessarily have anything to do with "more sophisticated" evaluations. High quality evaluations occur when researchers adhere to basic principles and procedures. Sample size and statistical analysis have a role to play in the evaluation process but not in the "more is better" fashion.

What all this means is that "sophisticated" is not an appropriate term to apply to an evaluation. There will be no suggestions here that some evaluation procedures are more sophisticated than others.

This rejection of the notion of sophistication does not mean that some evaluation projects are not more complicated than others. Assessing a comprehensive program like Head Start is obviously going to be more involved than analyzing a local school's hot lunch program. "Complexity" and "sophistication" are not the same thing, and evaluators have to be sure they do not confuse the two.

Another point raised earlier concerns the question of why organizations put themselves through the trouble of a lengthy, frustrating, and often inconclusive research process. Could it be because going through this agony is the only way for these organizations to get money to support their activities? The federal government and most private foundations will not usually give money to an individual or organization unless there is an evaluation component included as part of the project. When someone hands out money, the organization has to be ready when people start asking questions about results. And someone will ask those questions.

The prevailing demand for "accountability" from programs has produced some of the interest in program evaluation. But there also has been a desire to have some understanding about the results of the social activities taking place. Comprehensive social programs such as Head Start have no product — at least not in the normally recognized use of the term. Children do not roll off assembly lines like automobiles, subject to a physical inspection and some type of quality control.

Although generally there are no profit statements to show whether a program is making money, this does not mean that financial concerns about social programs are completely neglected. Quite the contrary! Some social programs were started as a way of conserving money. But this notion of financial accountability is not the same as an intention of making a profit. But we will postpone a discussion of this topic and get back to the idea that there are other than funding motivations behind the recent increased interest in program evaluations.

In general, program evaluations are simply good business for everyone involved. When they are properly done, evaluations are effective and creative management tools. A good evaluation provides managers with practical information about inefficient procedures. Working in the middle of those activities every day, a manager may find it difficult to get a realistic picture of what is happening, good and bad, within the organization.

Most employees probably do a good job, but there can be a few people who do not work at acceptable levels of performance. Those few people can compromise the whole operation. Similarly, most of the internal procedures of the organization might be working well, but they may be hampered by a few cumbersome practices. It would not take many of these wasteful procedures to foul up the operation of even a largely efficient organization.

Evaluations can also help managers by directing attention to a program's weak spots. Most social programs have no easily visible output. It may be impossible for any but the most dedicated manager to find out who and what is working to capacity. A comprehensive evaluation provides the kind of information managers can use to detect where their weak spots are and possibly how to go about fixing them.

An evaluation can also document structural weaknesses, especially when there are confused or nonexistent organizational lines of authority. It is not unusual for social service organizations to get bogged down because of obscure lines of authority or responsibility. This can happen even to profit-centered organizations. When a program grows quickly, the organizational lines can fade or blur to the point where employees do not know who is supposed to be doing what. Evaluators can document these weaknesses.

Finally, and not incidentally, an evaluation can be a source of inspiration for new ideas. New ideas can come from people who look at a situation with a fresh approach. Most evaluators develop "feelings" about the programs they study. Drawing on their experiences from similar settings, researchers often have ideas that may offer the potential for dramatic changes in an organization's performance. The viewpoint of someone from the outside is frequently invaluable.

But even if the evaluators' suggestions are rejected or if they do not have dramatic results, those recommendations can still be the catalysts for internal creativity. Ideas for changes within organizations have a way of being contagious, and once the evaluators start things going, new ideas may come in a stream.

The potential policy implications of program evaluations are also important, a point mentioned earlier. If the Community Crime Program studied by the accounting firm had been successful (which it was not!), the federal government might have redirected some of its law enforcement budget to similar activities throughout the country. Just as a high profit margin for a company can do wonders for a particular product line, a highly successful evaluation could influence social policy. Although the notion of "what is good for General Motors is good for the country" is not necessarily appropriate, it is still reasonable to argue that what works in New Jersey might also be successful in New Mexico.

Finally, and perhaps the most overlooked argument in support of formal program evaluations is the idea of what would happen without them. There is no other objective means for assessing the effectiveness of social activities.

Almost as soon as programs emerge, and certainly after they set up their activities, they develop constituencies. Newly hired employees and program participants form the core of interest groups supporting the new program. Depending on the nature of the activities, additional support could also come from a variety of professional associations and ethnic or religious groups and from those citizens for whom no cause is too small. All these groups could be expected to support the continuation of a program, especially if there is no negative performance record to argue against that continuation.

On the other hand, an effective program may disappear because of the presence of strong opposition. Some of these potential adversaries come from groups whose own programs were cut. These individuals are understandably upset, and they can take their frustrations out on people and programs that are still operating.

Other opposition could originate from professional associations. Ethnic or religious groups with strong reservations about certain activities often appear on the scene, as do a variety of people with strong ideological reservations about what is being done.

Both groups, supporters and opponents, have strong opinions about their respective positions on the social program in question. Their opinions are often stated forcefully, and on occasion, with some eloquence: "This program is doing wonderful things for the community. I can see the results every time I go into the neighborhood – the smiles on the faces of the children, the happy couples in the park. We cannot deprive our citizens of this vital service!"

That appealing description tells the story from one side. The opponents on the other side will rebut those glowing testaments with opinions of equal intensity: "This boondoggle is a waste of the taxpayer's money. Nothing has changed in the community. The program serves the needs of only a few bureaucrats, and it harms the people it was supposed to help!"

It is hard to believe the two sides are talking about the same program. The only thing the groups have in common is the strength of their convictions. Those "convictions" are rarely grounded in anything other than a deeply held belief that the other side is wrong. Supporters on both sides of the ideological battle often lack substantive information on how the program is doing, but the soundness of their opinions is beside the point. Their convictions are almost sacred, and their minds, once made up, are not going to change easily.

The rest of the general population (i.e., the taxpayers) is usually interested in facts. These other citizens want and need something other than opinion as a basis for assessing the worth of social programs.

9

No one, least of all the average taxpayer, enjoys "pouring money down a sink hole." But neither do these conscientious citizens want to get rid of programs that are doing good things. Deciding which program is a success and which is the sink hole requires data, not diatribe, and information, not innuendo.

This capacity for helping to produce sounder decisions about social programs is arguably the most important and the least recognized advantage to formal evaluation research. Program evaluation offers decision-makers some consistent and objective assistance in making judgments about social programs.

Better decisions, though, are not necessarily the "best" decisions. "Best" is a relative term. One person's best idea will be another person's worst nightmare. Even the strongest evaluation will not be likely to alter basic convictions about the desirability or the "evil" of particular policies. Evaluation research, for all its capacities, is only one of a number of potential influences on the decision-making process. Politics, economics, psychology—these and a few surprise ingredients usually influence decisions on public policy. It would be naive and incorrect to believe that decision-makers wait for the results of program evaluations before writing a law or signing the latest budget. While evaluation research has an important role to play, researchers should not delude themselves by thinking that their contribution is the most important one.

The evaluation process, even when it is done professionally, is not a perfect mechanism. There are always a few limitations with the process and some need to qualify the conclusions made. Even a thorough, well-funded, and perfectly executed evaluation cannot guarantee that subsequent decisions are going to be the "best" ones.

Overall, a professional program evaluation lends a structure of objectivity and precision to a decision-making process. In terms of making decisions about the utility of a program and the social philosophies underlying it, there is no adequate substitute for a formal evaluation.

Although the evaluation process is often long and can be somewhat complicated, it is a good idea to start out with a simple overview. Figure 1.1 illustrates the important steps in the evaluation process: This diagram of the "how" of an evaluation process shows the first step as a formalized "need assessment." It seems reasonable to expect that before the start of any new social program, someone establishes a need for the activity. It is possible to have a program that no one really needs; it is also conceivable for the needs process to work in reverse. An individual or group could devise a product or program and then try to show a need for it. If the need is not there, someone could even attempt to create it.

Figure 1.1 • *The Evaluation Process*

1. Need Assessment

2. Delivery Format

3. Program Activities

4. Outcome/Evaluation

The diagram illustrates what might be considered the "normal process." The examples that follow assume that the existence of a definite need is the first step in the evaluation process.

Somewhere in this country there is probably a city that has large amounts of money accumulating in its bank accounts. One day, the elected leaders of this municipality might decide to conduct a comprehensive community survey. Since the financial resources are available, they want to find out if their constituents are lacking anything in the way of governmental services. The officials look for any "unmet needs" within the community.

In addition to documenting these needs, the city officials may also have a few specific topics or services in mind when they design the survey. They may want to use the needs survey to find out whether the older people in the community could use a Meals on Wheels Program. They might want to know if local children need after-school activities and supervision or if a significant number of adult readers would benefit from longer community library hours.

Community "need assessment" surveys are one way of beginning the process that culminates in a program evaluation. A need assessment does exactly what the phrase suggests: it assesses what the specific needs are within a particular group or community.

As useful as it may be for documenting specific needs, a formal need assessment could have the unintended effect of "creating" a

11

specific need. It is not difficult, for example, to visualize citizens in that mythical city who, when asked if they needed a community activity center, would respond with an overwhelming yes! Why would anyone expect these people to say anything but yes? If these people did not get a community center, they might conclude that someone else will. Or the city will spend (their) money in some other fashion, for example, a new sewage treatment plant. So yes, they "need" a new community center. By the time the public debate finishes, it will be obvious to everyone that the community badly needs this center. It is fascinating, once a question arises about a potential community service, how quickly a "want" can turn into a strong and deeply felt "need."

Besides formal community surveys, there are less suggestive procedures for assessing the needs of a group or community. These other techniques can pose less risk of creating "accidental" needs. A community need could be spotted, for example, because of problems uncovered by one of the local agencies. Small children found wandering the streets by police during the day could be a sign that the community could use institutionalized day care for its working parents.

A stream of domestic violence cases treated in local hospitals could be an indication that a family counseling service might be appropriate. A feature report by a local newspaper on illnesses resulting from groundwater pollution could be the catalyst for additional community environmental protection programs. It is also not unusual for the federal government to pass legislation that informs local governments of local problems they may not have known they had.

However it comes about, and whether it is a formal or informal process, at some point there is usually a recognition that the community, or some segment therein, needs a specific service (Step 1). Assuming that the necessary financial resources are available, recognition of this program becomes a starting point for the selection or formation of a program to deliver those services (Step 2).

Though it might be necessary to create an entirely new agency to deliver those services, it is possible that adequate providers already exist. Perhaps some organization or government agency is performing a similar service. There could also be a small agency that is willing and able to expand its efforts. Either way, some agency or delivery system will have to be selected. At that point, a set of program activities designed to deal with the original need, whatever it was, will begin (Step 3).

The role of the evaluators usually begins after those program activities have gone on for some time. This delayed entry by the evaluators is not an ideal situation. Earlier consultations enable researchers to design program structures that strengthen and enhance their later assessments. Unfortunately, these early consultations with evaluators are rare. Someone usually calls evaluators only when it is necessary, that is, when it is time to (re)apply for a grant.

The role of the evaluators is to assess as well as they can whether the services and activities now in process are performed in the manner prescribed and whether they are having the desired effect (Step 4). The results of that evaluation presumably will be used to make appropriate modifications in the delivery system.

Before someone contacts evaluators, whether it is early or later in the process, there is a related issue that has to be resolved. This issue involves whether "internal" or "external" individuals will perform the evaluation. Should the evaluators be current employees, people who are familiar with the program and the organization? Or would it be better to bring in people from a professional research agency? Or perhaps a private consultant should be hired!

Each of these potential sources for evaluators has positive and negative aspects. Those who prefer insiders as evaluators insist, with good reason, that internal evaluators bring a thorough knowledge of the program to the evaluation process. Current employees do not have to spend time getting to know the program or the people involved. With this time saving, so the argument goes, internal evaluators can do a more thorough job, probably in less time, and with greater sensitivities to the unique characteristics of the program. Not incidentally, since they are already on the payroll, internal evaluators are also cheaper to use.

This last advantage, though it may be the most important for some financially strapped organizations, is also at the center of the objections often raised to using internal evaluators. The fact that they are "on the payroll" has implications that everyone involved needs to understand. Even if the individuals under consideration are highly qualified researchers, their status as current employees means that they are, potentially at least, far more susceptible to internal pressures than any external evaluators would or should be. In cases where they have had some direct involvement with the program being reviewed, these employees now serving as evaluators may have a personal interest in showing the program's positive side.

Even without direct pressures or personal interest, employee-evaluators know very well that the jobs of their coworkers and friends depend upon the receipt of continued funding. Collegiality can be a powerful and potentially disruptive force working against an objective evaluation from internal evaluators.

13

Even the absence of internal pressures is no guarantee that internal evaluators could be completely objective. It seems reasonable to expect that any employee called on to serve as an evaluator might carry a heavy load of existing biases into the evaluation process. These biases could be about people, office procedures, or work arrangements. Expecting total objectivity from people who are current employees seems almost unreasonable.

Objectivity versus understanding, high cost versus economy, the time periods needed, the ignorant outsider or the comfortable and accessible insider—reasonable arguments exist for the two approaches. In balance, though, the argument for using external evaluators seems more compelling.

Despite their *initial* lack of familiarity with the program being reviewed, external evaluators have one primary task when they come to the program site, and that is to find out how well a program is working. Outside evaluators may have a boss, but it is not the program manager. Outsiders rarely, though admittedly there could be exceptions, have any motivation to slant the evaluation in a given direction.

Even if the employee evaluators are assigned to their new duties on a full-time basis, with a new title along with those new responsibilities, they are still employees. They will be trying to do an evaluation, and the results of that activity may put them in a different position, either within the organization or with their fellow workers. Although many internal evaluators have accomplished their task competently and professionally, it is asking a lot.

Once evaluators have been selected, what exactly are they going to do? The next chapter will go over the more detailed steps that go into a program evaluation, but it would be useful to outline the more general characteristics that are part of the process.

A comprehensive plan is crucial. Early and careful planning is central to an effective evaluation. A variety of things have to be done in any evaluation, and it is easy for the smaller items to get lost in the process. Unless there is a master plan, with someone checking details, those small, forgotten items can coalesce into major headaches.

Rule 1: Plan the Evaluation Carefully

Having made the argument for a thorough plan, it is equally crucial, and not inconsistent, for evaluators to provide considerable flexibility in that research process. This flexibility is necessary, because there has never been a program evaluation that has come off precisely as planned. The characteristics of the participants change, a due date changes, budgets shrink, research activities that were once allowed are now forbidden because somebody changed his mind, and there are other things that change during an evaluation. If a new research plan is necessary every time a change occurs, the evaluation process is going to become a time-consuming nightmare.

Making a plan is important, and every evaluator ought to work from one. But those plans change, and the evaluators have to remain flexible, ready to respond to changes in the research atmosphere with appropriate modifications or alternatives.

Rule 2: Be Thorough

In every research situation, there are stacks of documents to be read, lots of interviews to be done, various program sites to be observed, and eventually reams of data to sift through and analyze. Initially, at least, the evaluators do not know which of all this information is the most useful or even which information is appropriate to use at all.

This initial uncertainty means that researchers have to examine virtually everything. Good evaluations, then, have to be thorough. Researchers have to review the available information to insure that they are using whatever is appropriate. They frequently have no control over the time or the financial resources allocated to the research process. Many times an agency will bring evaluators into a project at a late date and tell them to simply "put something together as fast as you can." In this kind of situation, the only option for the evaluators is to be as thorough as the circumstances permit.

Finally, every program evaluation should be set up so that potentially important information has the possibility of surfacing.

Rule 3: Keep the Research Process Open-Ended

A good evaluation needs to have *open-ended* capability in its design. "Open-ended" means a capability for obtaining information that no one, even the evaluators, initially expected to use. This serendipitous research capability provides some assurance that important information, even it it was unexpected, will have the opportunity to emerge.

In the Community Crime Prevention Program, the evaluators' design would have included provisions for gathering information on every important variable. But even with careful planning, it is possible that the evaluators neglected to consider collecting data on some important items.

15

Perhaps family stress was lower as a result of this program, because people were no longer worried about the crime on the streets. No one thought about family stress as a potential effect of this program when the evaluation was first designed, but it could turn out to be one of the program's most important effects.

The school grades of students in the community might also get better because they can concentrate more on their studies. Maybe no one thought about getting data on school grades. And it is possible, too, that improved academic performances are one of the program's primary accomplishments.

Omissions of research focal points during the planning phase are common. But they do not have to be fatal to the quality of the evaluation, as long as the data-gathering process has an open-ended capability that enables researchers to respond to surprises. The open-ended capability means that data on items such as family stress and student grades can emerge. How is it possible for those items to emerge when no one anticipated them?

Providing for the unexpected in the evaluation process is not as difficult as it may sound. The evaluators only have to provide the means for people, usually program employees or participants, to have the chance to tell what they know or what they are experiencing. Or there is an opportunity for the researchers themselves to discover a relationship they may not have been looking for. It is as (deceptively) simple as that. Flexibility in the research process means that the evaluators could adjust and begin collecting data on these potentially significant elements.

Finally, it is essential that all elements of the evaluation be value-free.

Rule 4: Be Objective

A good evaluation has to be objective, from its basic design through the final analysis. This objectivity throughout the process, in collecting the data, in analyzing the data, and in interpreting it, is absolutely essential. If it is possible for any critic to show evidence of bias, either from the evaluators or from the project design, then whatever value the analysis may have had will be lost.

It is not difficult to instill objectivity into the research. For one thing, the evaluators should generate data from as many sources as possible. It is difficult to indict the evaluators' interpretation when corroboration from a variety of sources is available.

Although it is important for the evaluators to rely on measures that are familiar and to gather enough data to support the interpretations, probably the most important guard for objectivity is to expose the evaluators' interpretations to as complete and thorough a discussion as possible before a final report is written. These discussions can reveal the weak links. The result of these corrective procedures will be a thorough, well-grounded analysis that meets any reasonable person's test for objectivity.

A program evaluation, then, should be well-planned, flexible, thorough, open ended, and objective. This is an impressive list of requirements, but it is only a start to a good evaluation. What are the specific steps in constructing a good evaluation? We will deal with that critical question in the next chapter.

Selected Readings

Hoover, K. R. (1988). *The Elements of Social Scientific Thinking*. New York: St. Martins.

A classic, and a real treasure of insights, especially for the research novice. It deals with some important issues in an informative and accessible fashion. This book would be a good tool for the individual looking for general background in social science research.

Kuhn, Thomas S. (1970). *The Structure of Scientific Revolutions*. Chicago, IL: University of Chicago Press.

Provides a readable view into the nature of scientific change.

CHAPTER TWO

A Step-by-Step Approach to Program Evaluations

Even experienced evaluators get frustrated and sometimes discouraged when they first look at the size and potential complexity of a new research project. A large social program with many activities, hundreds of employees, and stacks of internal documents can overwhelm the most enthusiastic researcher. Smaller programs have frustrations too, because reduced size is no guarantee of simplicity in evaluation projects. No matter what the program's dimensions, evaluators go through the same general process when they examine a program's activities.

For both novice and experienced researchers, the most practical and efficient way to conduct an evaluation is to approach it systematically, as a series of generally logical and carefully implemented steps. Complexities often disappear when researchers break the large task into more manageable stages.

This "one step at a time" approach has a lot of advantages. Primarily, it gives evaluators a sense of control over the many things that have to be done during a comprehensive program evaluation. That sense of confidence can be instrumental during the lengthy evaluation process. The only real drawback to this strategy is the possibility that working on those various smaller steps could cause evaluators to forget about the project's primary focus. The evaluators get involved, for example, in the complexities of the project's first phase. They do not start thinking about the second phase until they are finished with the first one; only then perhaps do they begin thinking about step two. It is time to look at step three when the second step two is completely finished. And so on.

One thing at a time. It makes sense, but eventually the evaluators' actions resemble those of individuals who are trying to watch every step they take. People who walk like that usually end up tripping over their own feet. Evaluators then have to be careful that all the attention on these individual steps does not have them tripping over their own research feet.

Evaluators can concentrate on these various steps in the process without losing their research focus. The broader vision simply requires an awareness that those various steps along the way are not self-contained entities but parts of a unified whole. Each step influences what comes after it in much the same way as what came before affects the current procedure. The whole process is like a cake recipe. In baking, the successful outcome depends on the proper completion of each step. Skip a step or do it improperly and the product will suffer.

Comparing a program evaluation to a construction project is another way of illustrating the way this research builds brick by brick. When building a home, you must start with a solid foundation. The flooring comes next. Then the walls are framed in, and finally the roof is put in place. Each step in the process has its own requirements as well as making a contribution to the overall structure. If the builder neglects something during one of those steps, the omission will affect the success of what follows. If the foundation is solid, the rest of the structure is more likely to be sound as well. A weak foundation, on the other hand, will generate problems for the home no matter how straight the walls or how perfect the roof.

An evaluation project has many similarities to a home construction project. Instead of wood and nails, researchers' tools are data-gathering procedures and analytical techniques. In both types of activity there is a right way to do the job. Although some variation in procedures during the construction is permissible, the participants have to pay attention to doing things the proper way.

The entire series of procedures or steps in the evaluation process is mostly logical, but "logic" is not always the ideal guide in determining the timing for implementation of these steps. Every evaluator has personal stories about an episode during a project that required unique adaptations. Most evaluation projects have something unique about them, whether it is the nature of the program participants, the type of program, or the setting itself. These varying characteristics often mean that the evaluators have to adjust either the timing or the content of those "seemingly logical" research steps. But if the researchers know what they are doing and why, and as long as they stay focused on the overall evaluation, these periodic adjustments do not have to turn into structural weaknesses.

With those general points in mind, we are ready to take an initial look at how a program evaluation is done. The same (hypothetical) Meals on Wheels social program will be the focal point throughout most of the discussions. Emphasizing one program obviously eliminates the value that could come from using different examples, but that disadvantage is offset by the ability to focus on the "internal logic" of the evaluation process.

A Case Study in Program Evaluation

A medium-sized city contacts a professional evaluation team and asks them to conduct an assessment of the city's Meals on Wheels Program. Several years earlier, the city introduced a Meals on Wheels Program (MOW) to provide regular home-delivered meals to its needy senior citizens. The program has been operating for about two years and receives funding from federal, state, and local sources. The community's application for renewed federal funding has stalled. The federal government informed the city that its pending application will not be processed until it submits a formal program evaluation.

Although the federal government warned them about the problem several months ago, city officials did not contact the evaluators until recently. After recognizing the time problem, the city officials promised the researchers unlimited cooperation and whatever funds within reason, that the evaluators needed. Unfortunately, because of the deadline for the federal grant application, the evaluators have only sixty days to complete the research and file their report.

There is probably not enough time for the kind of thorough process the evaluators would normally design. The evaluators make that point in a meeting, but the city officials have no options with the time period. An extension in the government application deadline is apparently out of the question. So the evaluators agree to do the best job they can under the circumstances.

Early the following morning, the research team plans the evaluation. At the end of what turns out to be a longer day than anyone intended, they finished the outline of their initial research plan. Everyone agrees that the research design is as good as it could be under the circumstances.

The overall plan is sound, although it lacks specifics in many phases of the coming investigation. But there is a good reason for this absence of detail. The evaluators do not want to restrict themselves to specific procedures until they have the chance to get into the field and familiarize themselves with the program and its activities. The researchers agree that with the time constraints placed on them, the initial design plan should stay flexible. The plan is as thorough as it can be. Everyone is ready to get started.

Step 1: Background Research

The first task in an effective program evaluation is for the researchers to get a working understanding of the program. Acquiring this background normally takes considerable time, especially when the evaluators are new to the situation. Establishing an adequate background, though, is worth whatever time it takes, even when time is short.

The evaluators need information on background items such as when the program started, and why. These basic details familiarize evaluators with the program and its origins. Later in the process, that information might be helpful.

This meals program focuses on the "needy elderly." As part of their background investigation, the researchers need to find the definition for "needy" that was used by the program designers. An understanding of the major program concepts acquired in this background phase will be helpful later, when the evaluators select measurements and data-gathering instruments. This kind of information is also important when the evaluators interpret the data.

Since it is usually impossible at this stage to know exactly which background items are going to be useful, it is a good idea to gather as much information as possible. The time allocated to this task depends on how much information exists, how much total time is available, and how many people are working on it. With this MOW program, getting a good background should not take an inordinate amount of time; two or three days will probably be enough. If it turns out that the evaluators need additional information later in the investigation, they can probably go back to their sources with additional questions.

At this initial stage, the evaluators are trying to find out everything possible about the meals program. This discovery process means looking into the circumstances surrounding the program with the zeal of investigative reporters. The goal of learning "everything" is probably too ambitious. Selectivity in this learning process is usually necessary. As a rule, though, it is better to have too much information than too little, and evaluators should not start the "weeding out" process until it is necessary.

When this background search is finished, the information should equip the evaluators to answer some important questions about the program. Where did this Meals on Wheels Program originate? Was it the result of local government legislation, or did the city do a formal needs assessment? What were the political, social, and economic issues that emerged during the initial debates? Did any individuals or groups play instrumental roles in promoting or opposing the program and, if so, who were the key individuals within each of these groups?

What was the initial intent of the program? Providing hot meals for needy senior citizens was the stated program focus, but it is possible that the program's real intent was something other than hot meals. Perhaps someone used this meals program as a vehicle to provide employment for community residents who were having difficulty finding jobs.

There is nothing sinister about hidden motives. In this situation, maybe the only way a jobs program could get funding was by "disguising" it as a senior citizens entitlement program. The evaluators' job is always made more difficult if these hidden agendas exist. But they do exist, and it is important for the evaluators to at least try to understand them. An evaluation is going to be more effective if researchers understand the real circumstances behind the program. Evaluators are looking for accuracy, not scandals.

The background investigation should also provide details about how the program operates organizationally. Who is in charge of what? And who reports to whom about what? Organizational dynamics are an integral part of the functioning of any enterprise, and they are also an important element in the analysis of a program's performance. Exceptionally good social programs have failed because of poor organization. On the other hand, more than a few poor programs have survived because of good organization. The evaluators have to spend time understanding organizational structure. Problems or weaknesses with organization often explain patterns that emerge later in the analysis.

In looking at these organizational dynamics, the evaluators should distinguish between the "formal" and the "informal" organizational structures. A published "Table of Organization" for this city meals program, for example, might look like figure 2.1.

This organizational chart seems to make the lines of authority clear. The mayor is responsible for everything and everyone in the city administration. The commissioner of human services handles the cities' social programs, and the director of the meals program presumably reports to the commissioner. Each individual site director in turn reports to the meals program director. The organization chart looks reasonably efficient in terms of who reports to whom and who apparently is responsible for what.

Figure 2.1 • *Metropolis Organization*

There is often a difference, however, between what is supposed to be and what is. After talking to the people involved, the evaluators discover that the commissioner of human services rarely has anything directly to do with the programs under her jurisdiction. Her executive assistant, a position that does not appear on any formal table of organization, actually handles the daily supervision of social programs.

Responsibility for the daily administration of program sites rests on the various administrative assistants of the site directors, who seem to be doing "other things" for the city. Here, again, there is nothing sinister about this situation. In this case, an "informal" organizational structure emerged to handle duties that the formal structure could not or would not handle. Virtually every large organization and small ones as well have these informal structures, and many managers seem happy with the situation. Informal operations are often the most efficient way—and sometimes the only way—organizations have for getting things done when normal procedures prove too cumbersome or too rigid.

Most executives and managers know about these shadow organizations. Many implicitly encourage those informal lines of communication, since they are often the best way, even for managers, of getting things done quickly. So, when evaluators assess an organization, it is important that they find out what goes on both formally and informally.

Another important background item concerns the "target population" of the program, the group that is presumably the reason for the activity. Evaluators need to know specifically who the intended recipients of the program services are. The target population in this case is the "needy elderly," because the city's grant proposal specifically mentioned that group.

The term "needy elderly" is reasonable, but it is not specific enough for the evaluators' purposes. For one thing, how do the program managers define the term "elderly"? Do they count all individuals over the age of sixty-five? Or do they use the age of seventy-five? The parameters used for the category will make a difference in determining the number of residents in the city who fit into that grouping.

The number of people considered "needy" is going to be even more difficult to define, but it is essential to find out how the program designers defined that term. The criteria for being "needy" is not the same everywhere. Some communities may define needy as having an annual income below the federal poverty line. Other communities may use a more practical measure, such as simply asking individuals whether or not they go to bed hungry.

It is important then that the evaluators understand how the program designers defined the key concepts. A primary ingredient in assessing a program's success is the degree to which that program services its target population. If the meals program, for example, serves one hundred elderly people every day, the evaluators have to know if this figure represents a successful performance.

If there are 120 needy elderly in the community, then it would be fair to say that the program is doing a good job of servicing its target population. On the other hand, if the community has over one thousand needy elderly, then the interpretation about the program's performance might be different. Learning the parameters of the key terms is obviously essential.

The initial step in the evaluation process is not finished until evaluators know what the meals program is and what it is trying to accomplish. Background information can also help with other parts of the research process. For example, since the meals program serves the needy elderly, it is possible that many of these people suffer from significant physical limitations. That information could be helpful when researchers consider data-gathering techniques.

A mailed questionnaire probably would have limited value as a data-gathering technique for this type of program. Many of the participants might have trouble reading or completing the document. So at this early point, then, the evaluators can begin considering other data-gathering possibilities.

How will the evaluators get background information on items like target populations and the characteristics of individuals involved in the program? Unfortunately, that information rarely comes in one handy package. Evaluators usually have to use two, three, or even more sources, depending on the kind of information needed and how accessible it is.

One important source is personal interviews with the individuals who played major roles in the formation and administration of the program. The list of potential interviewees includes the current and previous program directors, members of the board of trustees, if any, and the writer(s) of the initial grant proposal.

No matter how many interviews are conducted, it is essential that the evaluators keep a precise record of those interviews. The record could be made with an electronic recording device or by writing out *exactly* what the evaluators asked and precisely what the interviewees said. Recording information applies to interviews, personal observations, and whatever other interactions the evaluators may have with individuals during the project. This documentation will eventually serve as the basis for the analysis.

Often neglected are people who were once associated with the program but who have since departed. An angry employee who quit, a director who got fired or who left to take another position, individuals who no longer receive the services — all these people have information about the program. They may also be more willing to share their insights because they no longer have a current interest in the program. Although their comments and interpretations may be dismissed as "sour grapes" because they are no longer associated with the program, evaluators should not ignore the potential value of these interviews. Assuming there is enough time, evaluators should talk to any individual who has something important to say.

Official records and documents are another major source of background information. Depending on the extent of public discussion before the introduction of the program, there could be many appropriate documents. Those documents, including published minutes of official meetings and agency annual reports, can be a potential treasure chest of insight into the dynamics of the program's origins.

Census publications have considerable demographic information, and this material could be helpful background data for the evaluation. The evaluators could use census data to contrast the characteristics of this city's elderly citizens with their peers in other parts of the country.

Since in this case the city is applying for renewed funding, there is an initial grant proposal somewhere. Virtually any program that receives funds from a government agency or private foundation has had to submit a formal grant proposal. Evaluators should assign a high priority to obtaining a copy, or copies, if several such proposals were prepared over the years. Grant proposals provide useful background and detailed information about items like proposed budgets that may not be obtainable elsewhere.

Although formal grant proposals are sources of background information, evaluators have to use the information in these documents cautiously. Grant proposals are written to satisfy the requirements of funding agencies, and evaluators need to remember this point. People will say almost anything when money is at stake, and it may be that those early promises were less than realistic.

Finally, researchers can often obtain a significant amount of background material from the local media. Editorials, letters to the editor, feature reports on radio or television — these media sources can provide considerable information about what various influential members of the community were thinking and saying about the program. Although the program might appear noncontroversial, its formation may have generated significant public concerns: fear of traffic congestion; increased potential for exploitation of the elderly; and opposition to the allocation of additional tax monies. There are reasons for opposition even to a program that appears to be noncontroversial. The nature and strength of that opposition could play a role in what the program is doing now, and evaluators should be sensitive to those possibilities.

The volume of potential background resources that evaluators could explore might require the research team to be somewhat selective about which items to look at carefully. Particularly when time constraints exist, evaluators should not feel guilty about brushing lightly over some items. Although the goal in this first stage of the evaluation project is to learn as much about the program as possible, it is not possible to consider everything.

Step 2: Specifying the Program's Goals

Evaluators must accomplish two things in the second phase of the research process. First, they have to find out the specific goals of the program. This, of course, assumes that goals actually exist. If they do, then the evaluators must determine what, if anything, the program is doing to achieve those goals. There may well be more work here for the evaluators than is apparent initially.

Goals are statements of intentions. They are promises made about what the organization intends to accomplish with its efforts. Although goals should be a part of any organization's guiding philosophy, many do not have this specific focus. Some organizations may talk or write eloquently about their intention to "improve people's lives" or "make things better in the community," but these ambitious (and vague) statements do not provide much direction for program managers or evaluators.

In those cases where a program has no goals, it is the evaluators' task to provide them. And even when those goals exist, as they do in the Meals on Wheels Program, the goal statements may be useless for evaluation purposes. The meals program federal grant proposal, for example, lists two goals:

1. Help the elderly feel better about themselves.
2. Improve the lives of the elderly people in the community.

Although it would be difficult to argue with the nature of these intentions, evaluators will have a difficult time translating them into measurable goals. What does "feel better" mean? Is it a physical, psychological, or economic state?

The first task of the evaluators here is to modify these goals. They have to decide how these vague statements can be reworked to be specific and still reflect the intentions of the program designers. The key question in reworking these goals is how much improvement in people's lives is necessary before the program can be considered successful? Is a 10 percent improvement enough? Or does the program need to achieve a 25 percent improvement in people's lives before it is deemed successful?

These questions may sound petty, but they are not. The examination of a program's goals is an important element in its assessment, and judging those goals fairly requires the use of statements that are both precise and reasonable. It is not always easy to achieve both.

After a group discussion coupled with a review of the appropriate literature, the research team changed the wording of the two program goals. The modified intentions of the Meals on Wheels Program as they would be examined by evaluators now read as follows:

1. Achieve a 20 percent improvement in the sense of psychological well-being exhibited by the program participants.

2. Decrease by 25 percent the number of community elderly going into long-term care institutions.
3. Reduce the amount of personal stress within the families of the recipients by at least 25 percent.

The modifications in goals made by the evaluators changed the two somewhat vague goals into three more-precise statements. These specific intentions are the kinds of definitive statements that evaluators can use to measure a program's effectiveness.

Though the wording of the goals changed, the statements still represented the Meals on Wheels Program's stated or *explicit* goals. Explicit goals are the expressed intentions of the program, or what the program directors said they were going to do. Ideally, this list of a program's intentions would include every outcome that could be reasonably expected to come from the program. If the list of goals is sufficiently comprehensive, the evaluators have only the relatively simple task of working their way down the list.

A comprehensive list of goals is rarely found. Most of the time, the goals listed by the originators of a program are vague, incomplete, or both. Program designers often omit items that could represent important (potential) results of a program. These omissions are usually unintentional.

When the Meals on Wheels Program began, it is likely that no one directly involved with the program had enough information to predict all of the program's potential effects. These people designed an activity to provide a service for elderly people who were not getting proper nutrition. The organizers felt, with good reason, that delivering meals once a day would affect the psychological disposition of the participants and, to some extent, their families. The program was not expected to do anything else.

On occasion, it takes an outsider, someone with a fresh and informed perspective, to realize that a program of even limited scope has "side effects." Properly documented, those side effects could be an important element in deciding the ultimate success, or failure, of a program. Is it reasonable to not only list but examine these so-called side effects? The answer is an unqualified "yes!"

The rationale for examining these "implicit goals" is not to impose additional burdens on the program, but to provide a more comprehensive and ultimately a more effective evaluation. Even if the designers did not intend that their program would accomplish these other things, they are a legitimate part of the program's accomplishments.

Evaluators can use several sources to determine a program's implicit goals. One important source is the researcher's professional experience and expertise. The evaluator may have examined similar programs on other occasions and found that certain programmatic effects appeared in those instances. So it would be reasonable to look for those same effects in this situation.

The evaluator could also use the results of evaluations done on comparable programs operating in other cities as a basis for specifying additional tasks. If certain effects came from a Meals on Wheels Program in another large city, it would be reasonable to look for the same results here.

Finally, the professional literature is often a good source for determining program goals. In looking through the gerontological literature, researchers may find that when elderly people are given the opportunity to maintain greater independence because of home-delivered meals, they often get more involved in community affairs. With this information, it would be appropriate for the evaluators to list a "community involvement" index as an implicit goal for this program and to include some measure of community involvement to show the extent of this activity by the program's participants. If the people taking part in the meals program are getting more involved in community affairs, then this is another part of the story that is worth telling.

Goal analysis frequently involves more than listing explicit and implicit program goals. Important distinctions may have to be made between some of the statements on that list.

One of the potentially important differences is the "time frame" for a goal's completion. For example, it is possible to judge the success of some program goals almost instantly. If a goal of the Meals on Wheels Program is to "serve hot meals to at least 25 percent of the community's needy elderly within six months," evaluators could tell after six months whether the goal has been achieved. The time period for accomplishing this task is clear.

Other goals might not have obvious time periods. The reworked second goal for the Meals on Wheels Program states the intention to reduce the rate of institutionalization in the program population. The process of going into a long-term care institution is a complex and emotional decision. Some family situations may not get resolved for months, even years.

Although it is true that the availability of home delivered meals might equip many elderly people to stay out of institutions longer than they otherwise would, those results would not be likely to appear after only six months. So it would be unreasonable to use the same six month period to assess the success of this particular goal.

A longer time consideration does not mean that evaluators have to ignore certain goals. When an evaluation has to be done quickly, as is the case here, evaluators can provide the data and then emphasize that "an adequate assessment of this goal is not possible in the limited time frame available for this analysis."

Another potential complication in goal analysis is the existence of conflicting perspectives about what a program is doing. The Meals on Wheels Program may be doing wonderful things from the point of view of the city's elderly, but the effects of the program might not be viewed as wonderful by the people who own long-term care institutions. Keeping potential customers away is not something these institutions see as positive.

Finally, there are often more effects of a program than even a comprehensive goal listing can provide. A conscientious evaluator has to consider that possibility. Goal analysis is the beginning, not the end, of an effective program evaluation.

During the goal phase of the investigation, evaluators should also describe exactly what the program does to accomplish its goals. Ideally, a program has a set of activities oriented around its various goals. It can be unsettling if evaluators discover that a social program has several goals but no apparent activities connected to the realization of those goals. When a situation like this occurs, it obviously needs to be part of the evaluators' assessment and discussion.

Goals are often the first of several potential friction points with program managers. All of a sudden, the evaluator is looking at things that could present some problems. "You aren't going to hold us to that 25 percent figure, are you?" a program manager might ask. Goal statements made in order to get funded become unmet challenges or unfulfilled promises. No one likes to be told that they haven't kept a promise.

When they are asked about their program's goals, managers may become aware for the first time of the evaluation's potential implications. Their sensitivities should be understood. This awareness does not mean that evaluators have to respond to each concern. But they can assure the managers that the evaluation is not intended and will (probably) not serve ultimately as a job performance appraisal.

Managers can be told, for example, that the evaluator is not holding anyone to a specific standard. The evaluator assesses a program based on what the originators of the program said they were going to do—no more, but certainly no less, either.

Experienced evaluators know that even explicit goals are not promises carved in stone. They are the program's initial intentions, usually made in good faith. Many things may have changed since those intentions were written, and a consideration of these changes would be a part of the evaluator's comments.

Having said that, it is still not the job (and it could be the professional undoing) of an evaluator to "negotiate" the specific content of the program's goals. Once an evaluator decides that there is good reason for looking at a specific goal, that item should not be open to discussion or negotiation with the program's managers. Rewording a goal because of an evaluator's professional judgment is not the same as changing its content or ignoring it altogether because of internal or external pressure.

Program managers and other interested parties are free to dispute the evaluators' findings and interpretations. The structure of the evaluation though should be left to the professionals. That is, after all, why someone hired them. Evaluators who allow various interested individuals to restructure the research design are asking for trouble and for the challenges to the evaluation's objectivity that are sure to follow.

Determining a program's goals then is an important part of an evaluation. Goal analysis is not the entire evaluation, but it does represent an important beginning.

Step 3: Selecting the Research Design

There are three especially critical components of an effective evaluation. Selecting a research design is the first of the three parts.

A research (or evaluation) design is a schematic outline that lays out the timing of the data-gathering procedures. With an evaluation design, evaluators schedule the sequence for that data-gathering, a sequence that has implications for what comes later.

The following diagram provides one example of an evaluation design:

Pretest	*Program*	*Posttest*
01	X	02

In this simple design, evaluators plan to administer a pretest (01) before the program (X) begins. After the program is finished, or when the evaluation is complete, they administer a posttest (02). This basic design is a fairly simple one, yet it includes two components that are part of other, more complex structures. Most of the more complicated research designs are only rearrangements of these central components.

Pretests are measurements taken before the beginning of a program. They are useful because they provide a baseline or beginning point for the documentation of any change occurring because of program activities.

Posttests are measurements done at the conclusion of a program or at the close of the evaluation process. These later measurements are an integral part of assessing any changes that may have happened because of program activities.

Suppose that an evaluator is using a 100-point psychological well-being test to examine the performance of the Meals on Wheels Program. The data collected from these tests show the following pattern:

Pretest	Program	Posttest
01	X	02
56	—	82

These data indicate that the elderly people in the program went from an average score of 56 on the psychological test to a score of 82. The 46 percent improvement sounds like a considerable achievement for the program, but any reasonable analysis about a program's effects is not that simple. A conclusion about the success of the program based only on these data would be premature. The research design was not powerful enough to justify that conclusion.

Although a discussion of the relative strength of various research designs will come in the next chapter, it would be useful to define several other components used in evaluation designs.

Experimental groups include individuals participating in the program under study. The program participants are usually the people evaluators are most interested in, because what they do and say usually reflect the success or failure of the program's goals.

Control groups consist of individuals presumably similar in personal characteristics to those in the experimental group, except that these control group people are not participating in the program. Although the existence of control groups provides a potentially important basis for comparison, establishing a group that has "similar characteristics" can be difficult for evaluators.

If the Meals on Wheels Program serves two hundred elderly individuals on a daily basis and most of these people have significant health problems that limit their mobility, it would be necessary, if evaluators want an "ideal" control group, to locate two hundred elderly people with some health restrictions who are not getting Meals on Wheels delivery services. In all other respects, age, ethnic grouping, marital status, and so on, the two groups should be similar.

The problem is, Where would the evaluator find these two hundred additional people? It would not be reasonable to use residents in a nursing home, because institutional residents are receiving a complete range of services. Elderly people who come to a community senior center every day are an active and less physically limited group, so they would not be an ideal control group either.

The best comparison would be to locate several hundred needy elderly who have been cleared for but have not yet started to receive home meal deliveries. This would be as close to an ideal control group as evaluators are likely to get. Unfortunately, ideal control groups rarely exist, and evaluators frequently have to use the best control group available. If it turns out that the experimental and control groups have significant differences in important attributes, the evaluators' analysis has to reflect this disparity.

Experimental groups, control groups, pretests, and posttests — these four items are the major components in most evaluation designs. More needs to be said about the complexities of evaluation designs — and it will be said in the next chapter.

Step 4: Select the Measurements

Adequate measurement of the various items in the program's goals is the second critical leg of an effective evaluation. Without adequate measurement, any discussion about what may have happened because of a program's activities is speculation. Obviously, if evaluators use improper or inadequate measurements for the items in the Meals on Wheels Program goals, they cannot say much about how successful the program has been. It is apparent then that a program's measurements have to be selected carefully.

Evaluators are usually able to choose from several alternate measurements, but those options are rarely equal. For example, one item the evaluators have to measure in the meals program is "psychological well-being." The evaluators would first look for options within the professional literature. "Psychological well-being" is a common social science term, so there should be many studies with a variety of possible measures. The evaluators could also examine articles in trade journals. Wherever they look, they have to find measures that are valid, reliable, and suitable for the program's setting.

Valid measures are those that adequately measure the item in question. Reliable measures are those that show consistency. Documented assessments of both reliability and validity are part of any published professional study, and the evaluators should examine those assessments carefully.

The "suitability" of the various measures is a little trickier to determine because no standard index is available. The evaluators are looking for measures that are appropriate for use in a certain group or setting, and this changes from time to time and place to place. A measure for psychological well-being used in a sample of high school students, for example, might be totally unsuited for a sample of elderly people.

Another published measure might require an experimental setting, where the subjects come to a specified location and do a series of chores under the watchful eye of a researcher. It would be logistically difficult and perhaps ethically impossible to transport hundreds of homebound elderly to any such experimental sites. This particular measure then, whatever its merits, is obviously unsuitable for the meals program population.

Another alternative might require an expenditure of both time and money that the evaluators do not have. Despite its advantages, if a measure requires resources that aren't available, the project can't use it. So, although the process of measurement selection implies a choice, the number of alternatives may be less than evaluators might have initially thought.

There are some research situations when no adequate or appropriate measurements exist. In these situations, evaluators have no choice but to devise a new measurement. This situation is not necessarily bad, but it does introduce an element of uncertainty into the analysis. Undesirable though it may be, uncertainty with a measurement is usually preferable to omission.

Whatever the final decision, it makes sense for evaluators to spend an appropriate amount of time selecting the best measurement devices possible. Appropriate measurement is absolutely essential to an effective program evaluation. More will also be said about this critical process in the next chapter.

Step 5: Data Collection

Collecting the data is the third leg of an effective program evaluation. This phase of the evaluation process involves selecting the techniques and then actually obtaining the data.

Selecting the most appropriate technique for collecting information from a series of alternatives is not as difficult as it might seem. By the time the evaluator reaches this point in the research process, a considerable weeding-out of potential data-collecting techniques has already occurred.

For example, the measure selected for "psychological well-being" may require the use of a questionnaire. In this case, there is nothing to decide. Unless there is some compelling argument against it, a questionnaire has to be used. On the other hand, if the argument against the questionnaire is persuasive, evaluators may have to select a measure that allows the use of some other collection technique.

Once techniques have been selected, evaluators must begin the process carefully. Data collection usually puts evaluators in a potentially sensitive relationship with the program's participants and employees. Information gathering is the point in the research process when the evaluation becomes serious, at least in the minds of the individuals who are watching and waiting for the evaluators to finish.

The exploratory interviews are over, the newspapers have been reviewed, the grant proposal has been read, and now it is obvious to everyone that evaluators are gathering material that will judge "their" program. Program participants will want to know what the researchers are doing and how they plan to use the information. Employees will begin to ask what will happen once the evaluators submit their report. Managers start thinking about their jobs. Understandably, the potential for friction here is considerable. The evaluators' task is to minimize that friction by convincing everyone that data collection is only one ingredient in a lengthy and involved assessment process.

It is important for evaluators to match the various data-gathering procedures against the list of program goals to be sure that adequate information will be available. "Check twice, collect once" – this rule is a twist on an old building trade's dictum, and it is a good rule for the evaluator as well. No one wants to be in a situation where the final report is almost finished and someone discovers that "we forgot to get any data on psychological well-being!"

Although it is possible for evaluators to go back to the program sites to obtain additional information, these return trips and the

35

additional frustration they could bring (reactions like "What do they want now?") could easily distort the nature of the data and the quality of the evaluation. Avoid return trips by careful attention to details throughout the research process.

At some point in the data-gathering phase, evaluators have to decide if sampling is appropriate or necessary. In a small program, or in those cases where time and money are not factors, sampling procedures are not necessary—because the total population is small enough to collect data from everyone involved.

Often, evaluators work with experimental and control groups that are so large that they cannot collect data from everyone. Sampling would be necessary in these cases.

A sample is a portion or subgroup of the population. From the samples, researchers make generalizations about the entire population. Sampling is not necessarily a weakness in the evaluation as long as it is done properly. Although the nuances of the various sampling processes will not be discussed at length here, evaluators should insure that the sample collected is of adequate size and representative of the entire population.

The sample size depends to some extent on the size of the population. A statistical formula determines sample size. But the heterogeneity (or diversity) of the population is also important. The more diverse the population, the larger will be the "adequate" sample size.

Another important criteria for sample size is that it is large enough for the analysis the researchers want to do. If they want to compile percentages, for example, they need a fairly large sample size. A conclusion of a "20 percent increase" in a program's performance with a sample of only five people is obviously inappropriate.

Insuring a representative sample is a somewhat easier task. Representativeness comes from the use of a *random sample*. For evaluators to generate a random sample, every individual in the population has to have the same chance of being included in the sample.

If the Meals on Wheels Program is currently feeding four thousand people a day and the evaluators need a representative sample, there is not much of a problem getting it. This population of four thousand people is specific, and the evaluators can easily obtain every name. Researchers could put those four thousand names in someone's hat, shake it, and draw out a 10 percent sample of four hundred names. More likely they would randomly pick a starting point on that list and take every tenth name. Either way, it would be hard to conceive of a more ideal situation for randomizing a sample.

The problem in most research situations comes when a population group is not so clearly defined. How would an evaluator draw a random sample of local marijuana smokers? What about a random sample of Americans who have done some shoplifting? Or of citizens who have incomes they did not report on their tax forms? For many categories of behavior, there are no lists, no places where entire populations are defined. As a result, there is often no reasonable way to insure the presence of a random sample.

The problem posed by this potential absence of representativeness in a sample is that researchers have no way of being confident that their sample accurately portrays the characteristics of the larger population. In these cases, there is a potential for a biased or misleading sample group.

Several years ago, a community group planned to conduct a survey. They wanted to examine local attitudes on several political issues. To test the attitudes in the community, the research group decided to interview every fourth person going into the local food cooperative on a Monday morning. "Is that a good way to get our sample," the group asked?

As gently as possible, they were told, "No, this is not a good way to draw a random sample." It was not even close to being a good way. For one thing, only certain types of people shop at food cooperatives. As anyone who has been to a co-op can attest, the customers are not representative of the general population. Their mood is different from that of customers of popular chain grocery stores.

And by selecting Monday morning, those researchers introduced yet another bias into their sample. They would not talk to people with jobs that made it impossible to shop on a weekday morning. What they would generate from their survey is information from an unrepresentative (nonrandom) sample.

Nothing is wrong with a nonrandom sample as long as researchers know what they have and realize that the data may not be characteristic of the general population. Researchers should ask themselves the question, "What is this sample a sample of?"

Generalizations may be made from nonrandom samples, but they have to be made carefully. Although a nonrandom sample may generate helpful data, there is a *significant potential for distortion to be introduced into the data,* and researchers have to be sensitive to those possibilities.

On occasion, biases emerge even when evaluators least expect them. Like an errant spouse, biases can "sneak in" the back door. For example, as a means of drawing a sample of the meals program participants, the evaluators might decide to simply ask the program director for a complete listing of the participants.

"I already have a list of most of our clients," the director says.

Several days later, he provides a list to the evaluators. Although the director may only have been trying to be helpful, he ends up providing an internal list that "weeded out" chronic complainers. The director may have reasons for maintaining a more restricted list, but the evaluators would not. By using this sampling list, the evaluators generate data that do not represent the entire population. This weakness is a problem; but if the evaluators don't know about the weakness, that problem becomes a major structural deficiency in whatever analysis follows.

The moral of this illustration is, if evaluators draw a sample, they should supervise the sampling process. The importance of the sampling process warrants close attention. So, too, does the entire process of data collection. As the third leg in an effective program evaluation, data collection justifies the time and effort it takes to insure the availability of sufficient and accurate information. The next chapter provides more details about this essential procedure.

Step 5: Analysis

This is the stage in the evaluation when researchers organize the data to examine the program's accomplishments. A carefully structured analysis is also central to the success of the overall evaluation. Evaluators take the information generated by the data-gathering procedures and put it into forms that provide a reasoned and accurate assessment of the program's performance.

The analysis has to be thorough. But it also has to be in a form that is understandable to an audience that is not used to statistics. Although these goals appear to be contradictory, they need not be. A later chapter provides some important details about this particularly interesting phase of the investigation.

Step 6: Interpretations and Recommendations

This is the point where the frosting goes on the cake. Everything that has gone before, from the needs assessment to the selection of measurements and the analysis has been for one primary purpose—to provide evaluators with the tools to assess a program's performance.

All the interpretations and recommendations the evaluators make at this point draw on what has gone before. Did the Meals on Wheels Program improve the participants' sense of psychological well-being? Did it reduce family stress? Were the institutionalization rates lower among the populations that received these meals?

If the evaluators performed the steps properly, there will be a body of reliable information on which to base conclusions and interpretations. If the final report states that "there has been significant psychological improvement within the recipients of this meals program," the readers should find enough data in the report to support that conclusion. The quality of the measurement for psychological well-being and the nature of the devices used to collect the information should be enough to satisfy even the most critical readers.

If the evaluators suggest allowing more time for the drivers to distribute the meals, because this would provide time for informal conversation that is important to the program participants, they should have some evidence to support these suggestions as well.

Evaluations are frequently conducted in situations that are less than perfect. Many times, the evaluators made changes during the process, and some of those changes may have been significant. For example, the evaluation may have developed critical weaknesses when researchers had to change the scope of the data-gathering techniques.

More problems and weaknesses could have emerged when evaluators had to rely on new and perhaps inappropriate measures. They may have used a nonrepresentative sample. These kinds of research situations happen regularly.

Evaluators should be honest about weaknesses within the evaluation, making it plain, for example, that a certain measure is weak or the sample was not random. Then, although the final report describes an imperfect evaluation that is not as good as most people wanted, it will be an honest report. Methodological problems might foster conclusions sprinkled with qualifiers such as "it is possible . . . although the data are inconclusive, it appears that. . . ." These are not the kinds of definitive statements that evaluators want to make. But evaluators must opt for honesty.

These six steps are the framework for effective program evaluations. Although the steps progress in sequence, evaluators do not necessarily have to deal with them in this precise order. Some evaluators prefer to handle several procedures at the same time. Although not generally a good idea, this combining process can be more efficient. For example, the three methodological components, measurement, data collection and research design, could be handled at the same time.

Although the discussions of the three items were separate, there is an almost inextricable link between the procedures. Evaluators have to consider data-gathering procedures when thinking about measurement devices, and vice versa. And the nature of the evaluation design may affect the selection of the data-gathering procedures. The important thing to remember is not to regard each of these six steps as separate procedures in a rigid sequence. All the steps have to be done, but it is not essential that they are done in a specific order.

An ideal situation occurs when the research component is designed before the program starts. Bringing in an evaluator at an early point means that he or she could build evaluation procedures into the program structure.

For example, pretesting could be a part of the introductory process for program participants. They could fill out a questionnaire as part of the information-gathering process. Regular data-gathering would mean that the procedures would not pose any threat to the participants or employees. More importantly, managers would have ongoing reports, rather than periodic, and perhaps traumatic, evaluations.

When evaluation procedures are built-in, they seem to work very well. For example, a particularly effective evaluation procedure took place in a university cafeteria. Every day and at every meal, this cafeteria assigned one of the student workers to sit (unnoticed) at the end of the dirty-tray conveyor belt. The student kept a stroke tally of every item that came back uneaten to the kitchen.

At the end of each month, cafeteria managers looked at the accumulated data, and they had an excellent measure of unpopular food items. No one filled out any questionnaires, no one interviewed any people, and there were no worried cooks. This is a case where an effective evaluation process was built into the system. Small wonder that this college cafeteria was a great place to eat!

One final important note should be made about the evaluation process. The preceding discussions contain a number of references to limitations imposed by time and money. Although more time and money would not necessarily solve every evaluation problem, an ample supply of both helps researchers deal with most research difficulties. Effective evaluation research requires a considerable investment of both of these commodities. With adequate time and money, it is usually possible to conduct an evaluation that is thorough, comprehensive, and objective, and one that produces useful results. That such evaluations are not always done is often due not to errors by evaluators but to a lack of time or money. Individuals and organizations needing effective evaluations have to be prepared to provide researchers with an adequate amount of both resources.

This initial discussion of the evaluation process is only an overview. Now it is necessary to look more closely at some of the issues and procedures. A good place to begin is the three crucial ingredients of a good evaluation: data-gathering, measurement, and design.

Selected Readings

Cochran, W. G. (1977). *Sampling Techniques.* New York: Wiley.
>   This book provides an overview of the various sampling procedures. It is a good introduction into this essential process.

Kaplan, A. (1964). *The Conduct of Inquiry: Methodology for Behavioral Science.* San Francisco, CA: Chandler.
>   This text contains some informative discussions on a variety of important topics. Evaluators would be especially interested in the section on values and the role they play in the research process.

Royse, David. (1992). *Program Evaluation: An Introduction.* Chicago: Nelson-Hall.
>   A good overview of the evaluation process and an especially helpful section on the sampling process.

Simon, J. L. (1978). *Basic Research Methods in Social Science: The Art of Empirical Investigation.* New York: Random House.
>   This introductory research text is readable and covers issues such as validity, reliability, and sampling in some depth. The book also has an informative section on obstacles in the search for knowledge and how to overcome them.

CHAPTER THREE

The Methodological Components of Effective Program Evaluations

Chapter 2 established six steps to follow for an effective program evaluation. Though each step is important and contributes to the evaluation process, some of those steps are more vital to the overall process than others. Three steps in particular, those involving the evaluation design, measurement, and data-gathering procedures, have special significance. They are the methodological foundation for the rest of the evaluation structure.

These three components provide the tools that gather information about the program under study. That information ultimately is the basis for assessing the program. Unless the researcher collects that data properly, the evaluation will not have much substance or credibility. It makes sense, then, for the evaluator to spend whatever time is necessary to insure that these methodological components are as effective as possible.

The Evaluation Design

The evaluation design is a schematic "outline" for the project's data-gathering procedures. The design maps out the timing and arrangement of those collection procedures. The evaluators in effect set up a delivery route for the evaluation and mark the essential stops.

The primary components of evaluation designs are:

1. *Pretest*
   The pretest is the measurement taken before the start of the program. If evaluators intend to use pretests with the meals program, they would generate the measurements for items such as "psychological well-being" *before* participants got started in the program.

2. *Posttest*

   The researchers obtain this measurement either at the end of the program activities or when they finish the evaluation. When the time is limited, posttest measurements have to be planned and obtained promptly.

3. *The program*

   This term includes the complete range of activities performed as part of a social program. With the Meals on Wheels Program, it includes only the actual home meal deliveries.

4. *Experimental group*

   This category includes individuals who participate in the program activities. If the meals program feeds four thousand people a day, then every one of these four thousand people is, potentially at least, in the experimental group. With a group that large, it would be likely that the evaluators would rely on sampling to obtain the information.

5. *Control group*

   This category includes individuals not participating in the program. The performance of these people on the various measures is compared with those participating in the program. Setting up an adequate control group for the meals program requires evaluators to find a group of people almost "identical" to the experimental group. Ideally, the only visible differences between the two groups would be participation in the meals program.

The different arrangements of these components make up the shape and the relative strength (i.e., the power to make broader generalizations) of the various designs. The primary purpose of an evaluation design is to find out, as precisely and as accurately as possible, the effects of a particular social program (P). Evaluators then are trying to solve the following simple equation:

$$P > ?$$

What occurs as a result of the program's activities? Solving this question is the evaluators' central task. Coming up with an answer for that deceptively simple question requires, among other things, the use of a design that permits the researchers to screen out anything that could interfere with answers to that question. An ideal evaluation design is something like a tool for sculptors, something they could use on a block of granite to chip away anything that doesn't look like an elephant.

So it is with an evaluation. The researcher begins with a block of information and then, using the best design "tool," chips away everything that doesn't look like a program effect. In the meals program, the evaluators want to know the program's effects on the people receiving those meals. Do the deliveries improve the participants' sense of psychological well-being? Are participants staying out of long-term care institutions? Is there anything else happening as a result of these activities?

The obstacles to answering these questions are the other factors that influence individual behavior. Family visits, personal health, income, problems with home appliances, and a host of other incidental occurrences affect the participants, and the evaluators' chore is to sort everything out. The evaluators have to find some way of "screening out" these other influences. Providing the capability to eliminate those "outside" influences from the equation is the contribution an evaluation design makes—or can make.

It seems reasonable that evaluators would select the most powerful design, one that could screen out more of those other influences. The problem is that the decision about which evaluation design to use is often determined by other factors. Unique circumstances, limitations of resources such as time or money, and a variety of other problems usually mean that the evaluator's choice involves little more than selecting from a few alternatives.

In the current illustration, for example, the Meals on Wheels Program directors probably did not think about giving pre-admission psychological tests to the program participants. As a result, there are no pretest measurements available. The time is long past for giving these tests, so evaluators cannot use an evaluation design that relies on pretests.

The short time frame also means that if the evaluators want to use a control group, they have to compile one quickly. This necessity for haste probably means the use of a control group that is less than an ideal match for the program participants. Using a control group that is not a close match means that the evaluators have to be more cautious about generalizations.

No pretests, makeshift control groups—these difficult research situations unfortunately are common. So evaluators frequently have no choice except to work with weak designs and, as a result, with conclusions that are not as decisive as they might have been.

The meals program has existed for several years, and the evaluators want to know whether the food deliveries and the regular outside contact have affected the psychological well-being of the recipients. The evaluators decide to distribute a comprehensive questionnaire that includes a psychological profile. The questionnaire is identical to the one distributed to program participants two years earlier. The data are examined, and the comparison shows a 20 percent improvement in the psychological well-being of the meal recipients. The change is fairly dramatic, almost enough to have the program directors dancing in the hallways.

But any celebration would be premature. A lot of other things happened in those people's lives during the last two years. Any or all of those occurrences could have contributed to that sizable increase in psychological well-being.

For example, the federal government increased Social Security payments during the year. More money usually makes people feel better. The city started a fix-up program for homes belonging to older residents. Thousands of elderly people had their homes repaired at little or no cost to them, and this program could have had a positive effect. Finally, the metropolitan crime rate fell dramatically. All of these (non-program) events could have contributed to the positive changes in psychological well-being.

The passage of time also occasionally affects people's psychological disposition. Two years earlier, the city had more local problems. The country was in the depths of a severe recession, global unrest seemed constant, and a pervasive gloom had settled across the nation. Now, although not many of those conditions have improved, people are accustomed to the situation. Those problems, once new and worrisome, are now routine and no longer a cause for depression. Time heals all wounds, the old saying goes. Here, time might also be said to help people feel better about their lives irrespective of what else, like social programming, might have been happening.

This perceived ability to deal with the world might also have had some help from the research itself. Merely by asking people to fill out a questionnaire about their "sense of well-being" could exert an influence on their mental state.

A questionnaire is a "reactive" data-gathering instrument, called reactive because of the potential effects the procedure can have on people's attitudes and behavior. Filling out a questionnaire may actually change the behavior it presumes to study. When people answer questions about their psychological well-being, how they feel about themselves, the nature of their family relationships, and how they feel about the future, they may start thinking seriously about these issues, maybe

45

for the first time. They might wonder about their lives and what is right and wrong with them. Some people might alter their behavior after that thinking process starts—thus, the reactive effect! A person might think, "I never worried about not having many friends before. After I answered that question and I had to say that I didn't have any close friends, I resolved right then to change my life."

Of course, this is a contrived response to a hypothetical question, but it illustrates the point. Answering questions can be enough to influence people's attitudes. So evaluators who use reactive instruments as pretests have to think carefully about the potential influence those instruments may have. Actually, they have to do more than think about those influences; they have to try their best to screen them out!

When sorting out other influences, the evaluators have to consider the possibility that there was a "selection bias" operating when the program started. Perhaps a lot of media publicity gave older citizens the option of signing up for home meal deliveries. There were no eligibility requirements listed, other than being over the age of sixty-five. Under those circumstances, it is possible that some of the people who signed up were not exactly "needy."

Maybe the city wanted to attract more federal dollars for the grant, and they emphasized the need for high enrollment to the various municipal agencies. Every department, from the police to the sewer workers, may have recruited people for the meals program. As a result of this emphasis on head count, the program may now deliver many of its meals to people who are not even home to receive them. The recipients are out in the community, some of them even working.

If this is true, the evaluation of this program for "needy" recipients is going to be more difficult than anticipated. And unless the program data from the less-needy and truly-needy individuals can be separated, the data and the analyses are likely to be distorted to a significant degree.

Although there are an almost infinite number of these potentially distorting influences, fortunately the evaluators' job is to screen them out, not list them. Screening is the task of the design; the more powerful the evaluation design, the more of these "confounding elements" can be filtered out of the equation. The efficiency of the filtering process depends on the strength of the research design. The strength of that design generally depends on the number of comparisons.

Although the potential number of designs is large, indeed almost infinite, the essential points can be illustrated by looking at only a few.

The Single Group Pretest/Posttest Design

	Pretest	Program	Posttest
group a.	01	P	02

In this design, evaluators use both a pretest (01) and a posttest (02). The "01" and "02" designations refer to the measurements for the items being examined. If this first diagram applies to changes in psychological well-being, the designations (01 and 02) would apply to the average scores on the psychological test used to measure well-being.

Inserting hypothetical results for those psychological tests shows the following pattern:

	Pretest	Program	Posttest
group a.	48	P	72

The individuals in the meals program had an average score of "48" on the psychological well-being test before starting the program and an average score of "72" after two years in the program. The 50 percent increase is impressive, but as mentioned earlier, a celebration would be premature.

The reason for caution is that this design provides little conclusive evidence about the program's real effects. The design has only a pretest score to use for comparative purposes, so the potential for the presence of other influences on the change is considerable. The only thing evaluators know for sure from these data is that the well-being scores improved after participants had been in the program for two years.

Although it is possible that the Meals on Wheels Program is producing a large increase in positive psychological attitudes, it is also possible that other influences played some part in the change. Increases in Social Security payments made these people feel better too. So did the lower city crime rates. In fact, it is conceivable that the meals program is actually having a negative influence on individuals' sense of well-being, and the presence of those other positive items is disguising the program's psychologically destructive pattern. Doubtful though the latter interpretation may be, the point is that it is still difficult to determine what is going on in that program. With this first, very basic type of evaluation design, evaluators will not *know for sure,* because this design does not allow evaluators to screen out other possibilities. The meals program could have been responsible for all of the psychological improvement or it could have been responsible for none of it. The program's effects could also lie anywhere between these two points.

If more conclusive evidence is needed, the evaluators have to use a more powerful design, but stronger designs require the use of more comparisons. The evaluators have to be sure that these additional comparisons will be available.

The Two Group Pretest/Posttest Design

	Pretest	Program	Posttest
group a.	01	P	02
group b.	03	—	04

This design differs from the first one in that it contains additional scores from a control group (people who did not participate in the program activities). The introduction of a control group provides evaluators with two additional scores to compare. With these additional comparisons, evaluators can screen out *some* of the other potential influences on the effects of the program.

Inserting more hypothetical data from the psychological test shows the following pattern:

	Pretest	Program	Posttest
group a.	48	P	72
group b.	46	—	62

Now the evaluators have more information with which to assess the program. One item evaluators should look at right away is the scores of the two groups on the pretest. The scores are close (48 versus 46), indicating that the two groups started from the same point. If there had been a significant difference in the scores—if the control group score had been "22," for example—the difference might indicate that the two groups were different in some important ways. As a result, comparisons in posttest scores would be suspect.

Scores from the control group show that there was a significant increase in well-being within that group even with no exposure to the meals program. The experimental group had a 50 percent increase in their psychological well-being scores, but the control group had a 35 percent improvement. What once seemed to be a fairly dramatic improvement has turned into something less dramatic. And it is still not clear that the program can take credit for the ten point spread that exists between the two groups. Not yet, anyway.

The second design is an obvious improvement over the first one, but it still does not provide a firm statement about what the meals program is doing. Evaluators could have increased the power of the second design considerably if they had been able to randomize the composition of each group. This process, where older people from the entire elderly population of the city would have been assigned at random to one of the two groups, would have permitted evaluators to screen out a variety of other influences.

Randomizing both experimental and control groups makes a strong contribution to the strength of a research design. Unfortunately, it is rare that either program administrators or evaluators have this capacity. People are not often placed into social programs randomly. If an agency or program tried to randomize, even in the name of "good research," we would probably hear loud outbursts from many groups offended by the idea of manipulating people like players on a chess board.

It would be useful to understand how a randomization process for the Meals on Wheels Program might work. The first task in the process would be to obtain a listing of every needy elderly person living in the city. That list of perhaps fifty thousand people represents the total eligible population.

The city would randomly select four thousand names from this list. No rationale, no bias, nothing would be used to pick those names except a random procedure. Two thousand of those randomly selected names would be placed on the list to receive home delivered meals. The other two thousand people would act as the control group. The two groups would be virtually identical, except that one group would be getting the home delivered meals and the other would not.

The comparisons of the group scores would be a classic experiment, where the only difference between the two groups is the existence of the meals program. Hence, any difference in measured attributes, like the psychological well-being scores, could more reasonably be attributed to the program — assuming, of course, that the other elements in the research design were sufficiently comprehensive.

In situations where randomization is reasonable, it can provide a powerful tool in understanding a program's effects. The "problem" is that the randomization procedure is either not practical or not ethical — or a combination of both.

Posttest Only, Control Group Design

	Pretest	Program	Posttest
group a.	01	X?	—
group b.	—	X	02

Although this is not an especially powerful arrangement, it does show how researchers can alter the composition and structure of designs to fit unusual circumstances. Here, the researchers administered a pretest to a group of individuals. This pretested group may or may not be part of the program, but it does not matter.

Another group that did enter the program receives a posttest. The single comparison will be between the pretest score of the first group and the posttest score of the second group. This somewhat unusual process is often used when a pretest is considered especially "reactive."

The key to the appropriate use of this particular design is the *comparability* of the two groups. A close match in the characteristics of the two groups is important in order to make valid comparisons.

Evaluators who have the good fortune to be working under ideal conditions would be likely to choose to use the most powerful possible evaluation design. There is a research design that equips evaluators to make virtually unqualified generalizations about the program effects.

The Solomon Four Group Design

	Pretest	Program	Posttest
group a. R	01	P	02
group b. R	03	—	04
group c. R	—	P	05
group d. R	—	—	06

This design has everything to make an evaluator's heart sing. Four separate groups are used for comparisons—two experimental and two control groups. The randomization (R) of all four groups means that there is no selection bias to worry about. Elimination of the pretest in one experimental and one control group allows researchers to gauge the influence of any reactive effects coming from the questionnaire or from other potentially reactive techniques.

Putting in the psychological scores from the scores on that earlier test on the four groups shows the following pattern:

	Pretest	Program	Posttest
group a.	48	P	72
group b.	46	—	62
group c.	—	p	74
group d.	—	—	66

A comparison of pretest scores shows that the two groups taking the pretest were comparable on their psychological scores before the start of the program. The average scores of the two experimental groups (a and c: $\overline{X} = 73$) were larger than the control groups (b and d: $\overline{X} = 64$), but not by much. Comparing the two groups who took the pretest with those who did not indicates the possibility of some reactive effects from the use of a questionnaire. It appears at this point that the Meals on Wheels Program has a positive, if limited, effect on psychological well-being scores.

In some situations, though this is not common in social programs, evaluators might consider the use of a "double blind." With the use of a double blind, no one, not even the researchers, knows which individuals are actually involved in the experimental program. The use of this technique makes it impossible for anyone, including the evaluators, to unintentionally influence what takes place. Although the technique is more common to medical research, there could be a situation when a certain special program activity generated such strong feelings that using a double-blind procedure would be necessary in order to effectively evaluate the program. Obviously, the procedure would work only in situations where the individuals involved could not determine who was in the program.

Though only four evaluation designs are discussed here, there are more of them. Evaluators can use existing designs, or if necessary, they can design their own. They might want to design one that uses several control groups:

Pretest	Program	Posttest
01	X	02
03	—	04
05	—	06
—	—	07

Or, if the evaluators felt that the emergence of the program's effects was likely to be intermittent, they could use some form of a "time series design":

01   02   P   03   04   05   06   07   . . .

Evaluators should be willing and able either to modify existing designs or to design new ones. The only requirement with using any design is that the evaluators are aware of what they are doing and what they are going to get. This awareness means knowing the potential contributions of control groups, pretests, and the randomization process. The use of any design has no advantages if the evaluators do not appreciate its capabilities.

It is important to point out that every program goal has to be examined and *considered separately* for an evaluation design. This means that if a program has five goals, the evaluators may have to select five different evaluation designs. On the other hand, it is also possible that every one of the five goals can use the same design. Either way, there is no set pattern; selecting the evaluation designs is done on a goal-by-goal basis.

Although every goal has to be *considered* for a design, not every goal actually needs one. Researchers use designs to test for change or movement and then determine if they can attribute that change to the program.

If a program intends to improve scores on a psychological test, for example, this intent implies movement or change. In order to test the program's specific influence on any measured change, the researchers will use an evaluation design as part of the analytical process. The more powerful the design, the more definitive the evaluators can be about exactly how effective the program has been.

On the other hand, programs also have goals that are statements of simple tasks rather than predicted changes. Examples of tasks in the Meals on Wheels Program would include the following:

1. The meals program will serve hot dinners.
2. The staff will deliver the meals in sterilized containers.
3. Each driver will receive one week of training in conversational techniques.

The difference in these goals from those listed earlier is apparent. None of these latter goals implies any change in attributes or any direction in movement. Evaluators can sum up the results of these latter goals with a simple "yes" or "no." The program did it or the program did not accomplish it.

In these types of simple goal analyses, the evaluator does not have to provide a formal evaluation design because it is not necessary to "factor out" program effects from other, potentially confounding influences. In the case of some goals, there are no confounding effects.

The more elaborate designs require more comparisons. And those additional comparisons usually cost more money because of the additional data that are necessary. Program evaluators have to remember these things when they "select" their research designs.

The second leg of a program evaluation's methodological framework introduces some distinctly different problems for evaluators.

Measurement

The measurement stage is another crucial step in the evaluation process. The evaluators translate interesting ideas and ambitious goals into testable statements, something that can be a major and often frustrating task. Providing measures for every program component presents problems, because moving from abstract terms to definitive measurements is more difficult than it appears.

Suppose that a Meals on Wheels Program site director wants to evaluate a new delivery system. To measure how well the participants react to the new system, the director tells drivers to rate their own performance.

"But that is ridiculous," the director's colleagues insisted after she gave the details to them. "You can't use a self-evaluation system to measure how good the procedures are."

Yes you can! What her critics should have said was that self-evaluation in grading is an inadequate and unreliable measure. It is a measure—just not a very good one.

The example illustrates a central and persistent problem with the measurement process, namely, the difficulties involved in assessing the true nature of the item being studied. Measurements are not all the same; some devices do a better job than others. Some do no credible job at all. It is up to the evaluators to distinguish between the available measures, to assess their relative capacities, and then to use the best available one.

There are three criteria for making the measurement selection. First, measurements should have a high degree of adequacy, or "validity." Valid measures are those that accurately reflect the character of the attribute in question. If a measure is not valid, it does not have a strong relationship to what it presumes to describe. In that case, researchers can have no confidence in the data that come from this measure.

A high degree of validity, then, is an important attribute in measurement devices. Evaluators need to use measures that have the greatest possible validity. The greater the validity, the more confidence research-ers can have when forming judgments about a program's effects.

"Reliability" is another important measurement characteristic. Reliability (or consistency) in measurement means that under identi-cal circumstances, the measure shows consistent results. Suppose that a program director gives a psychological test to individuals at one pro-gram site. The group's average score on this test is 65.

The next week, before she can begin the new program, five new people arrive and are put into the program. So she decides to start over and administer the test again. The average score of the group the second time is 82.

For some reason, she administers the same test another time to the same group. The three test averages are 65, 82, and 96. If the test were reliable, those scores should have been the same or close to it. As it is, there is little doubt that the instructor has an unreliable measure of psychological health.

In any program assessment, evaluators have to be confident that the measures used will, under the same circumstances and with the same or similar individuals, yield similar results. Just as a scale that shows a person's weight as 167 pounds one day and 93 pounds the next would be considered unreliable (or broken), so too should an inconsistent measure be considered unreliable. Evaluators need mea-sures with high degrees of reliability.

Finding valid and reliable measures is often a problem. But some-times the problem is not as bad as other times. When a program's goals are relatively simple, for example, and the evaluator only needs information on personal attributes such as family income, educational level, and weight, measurement is generally not going to be a problem. In these cases, because proper measurement involves merely record-ing the information accurately, adequate measurement would not be much of an issue.

The measurement questions and problems occur when the evalu-ator has to deal with more complex variables. The third goal in the meals program focused on family stress. This variable is a good exam-ple of a more difficult measurement problem.

Family stress is a complex idea. What does "stress" mean? Re-searchers have to answer that question before they can locate an ade-quate measure. Stress could include factors such as psychological discomfort. If individuals are unhappy about their lives, that fact could contribute to whatever stress they feel. So the psychological discomfort of various family members should be a part of a stress measure.

The atmosphere in the surrounding community could also be contributing to the family's stress. If the members of the family feel isolated from or even afraid in their neighborhood, the negative atmosphere could also contribute to a high stress level.

The potential complexities in measuring something like stress are apparent. Fortunately, evaluators seldom have to be explorers when they need measurement devices. The use of the professional literature in their search is almost always helpful. So the first thing an evaluator ought to do is to review the appropriate literature. There are several good reference books devoted to measurement devices. These general sources provide evaluators with a starting list of measures used for particular variables along with documentation on the validity and reliability coefficients of each. If these general resources are not useful, published studies might be. The question for evaluators is often not "How do I measure this item?" but "Which one of these measures should I use?"

Using the literature does not free evaluators from measurement problems. The evaluators are still responsible for determining the validity and reliability of the various measures. But although high validity and reliability are important, they are not enough to justify using a measure. The circumstances in each research situation are different, and evaluators still have to determine the applicability of these measures.

In the meals program, for example, evaluators have some special situations: the program's participants have significant physical problems; there is no central location where people gather; and when the factors of different meals and different drivers are considered, each participant is really experiencing a "different program."

On such occasions, evaluators may decide to use an existing measure but only after making a few "minor" changes. Adapting a measure to fit the situation is acceptable, but before making any alterations in these measures, the evaluators should understand that the validity and reliability characteristics of that measure are not the same after those changes. Evaluators are creating a *new* measure. If evaluators make changes in the measurement, the potential for changes in the validity or reliability of the measure should be stated in the subsequent analysis.

One other element in the measurement selection process is the data-gathering technique used in the project. Some measures require the use of certain techniques. If evaluators have already decided that the cost of personal interviews is prohibitive, they obviously cannot select measures designed for an interview.

Adequate measurement, then, is a vital element in the methodology of the evaluation. Evaluators have to be sure of the validity, reliability, and suitability of the individual measures. It can be tricky to balance these requirements. But without adequate measurement, the rest of the evaluation, however good it may be, is virtually useless.

Data Gathering

Data gathering is the third critical methodological leg of an effective evaluation. Evaluators often have a number of options for gathering their data, but before looking at the strengths and weaknesses of the various techniques, evaluators have other things to consider.

For one thing, some techniques require more personal contact than others. This contact during an evaluation can generate special problems. The people involved in the program—the administrators, participants, and employees—know about the evaluation process. They often worry about what the evaluators are doing and what the results mean for their organization and for them as individuals. In extreme cases, where these concerns are strong, evaluators may have to consider using techniques that do not require much personal contact.

Being sensitive to people's concerns does not mean that evaluators have to change their plans every time someone is upset. But a recognition of individual sensitivities goes a long way in reducing the possibility of severe disruptions in the evaluation process. Evaluators have to do their jobs, even if it means that some people become irritated, but one of their goals should be to irritate as few people as possible.

The need for trained research personnel is another important consideration, especially if evaluators are hiring other people to do some of the data gathering. Some research techniques require more training than others. Interviews, for example, can be an extremely effective technique but only when done by competent people. If evaluators do not have enough skilled interviewers and if they do not have the time or funds to provide that training, they would be better off using another technique. A poorly done interview can produce more than bad data—it can generate a host of other problems as well.

Costs in both time and money are other considerations when thinking about the various data-gathering techniques. Some research techniques require considerably more time than others. As a result, they are more expensive. If time or budgetary considerations are important, evaluators may have to avoid a technique they would normally prefer.

In those unusual situations where time and money are not problems, evaluators might use several research techniques to generate information on each item. The use of several techniques of collecting data on specific items is called "triangulation." The process is a good way of increasing the level of confidence in the data.

An educational incentive program in a low income area of a large city illustrates the value of triangulation in the data-gathering stage. The program intends to increase the personal aspirations of high school students from low-income families. Through a series of lectures, site visits, and personal counseling, the program tries to motivate students to establish higher personal goals.

One way evaluators could test for changes in these aspirations would be a questionnaire that asks students whether they plan to attend college. A question about personal plans for higher education is only one way of getting at the answer. Students often respond to such questions in the way they are "expected" to respond, not in the way they really feel. If evaluators are not confident about the validity of the questionnaire data, or if they simply want corroboration, they could use additional techniques to generate more information on aspirations.

They might, for example, review the documents in the school office to see how many students requested literature from various schools, or how many individuals sent applications to various colleges. They would then have other, independent sources of information on student aspirations. If the measures were consistent, that is, if they showed the same pattern, conclusions about the effects the program had on personal aspirations would be stronger. When collecting data, more is usually better.

Another general consideration evaluators have is the "quality" of the data from the various techniques. Data quality is a slippery concept, and any five researchers are likely to come up with five different answers about which research technique provides the best quality data in a given situation.

Every researcher wants high-quality data. "High-quality" means that the researcher has information that describes the situation accurately. Poor-quality data does no one any good. The issue, then, is which techniques provide more high-quality data in a given situation. Evaluators must consider the idea of quality when deciding about research techniques.

Quality is not the only consideration in weighing a technique's relative merits. Researchers must also consider the characteristics of the participants, the nature of the research situation, and, as mentioned earlier, the types of measures used in the evaluation.

One other potentially important consideration is the need to include an "open-ended" element in the structure of the new data-gathering process. This capability for drawing new information into the analysis may not be vital in every situation, but if the evaluator is concerned about the existence of "unforeseen" items, it is useful to have this open-ended capability.

The evaluators of the Meals on Wheels Program may use a structured questionnaire to gather their information. Their questionnaire could be very specific, and the device would probably produce some useful results. But specific questions might not include *all* the effects of the program. For example, the program might be affecting the sex lives of the participants. The delivery of meals may give the recipients a greater sense of independence. That independence, in turn, may encourage the people to feel better about themselves. And that "feel better feeling" could be translating into a more active sex life. This scenario may be tenuous, but it could happen. If it did happen, the evaluators would want to know about it. They would probably not find out about the change in sex habits if they relied only on a questionnaire that contained very specific questions. Evaluators have to provide some openness in the data-gathering process to allow for discoveries.

Structured questionnaires seldom allow for this kind of insight. An unstructured interview is one way information about sexual encounters could have surfaced. Even an open-ended questionnaire could have done it, although it would be less likely. It is hard to imagine elderly people writing about their emerging sexual appetites on a questionnaire sent by an unknown individual.

With these more general considerations in mind, the evaluators are ready to examine the relative advantages and disadvantages of the various data-gathering techniques.

The Questionnaire

The mailed questionnaire is a commonly used research technique. Although some researchers criticize the quality of survey data, the technique remains popular primarily because it is one of the most convenient research techniques to use. Although preparation of a questionnaire can be a significant task, once it is written, researchers only have to mail it and wait for the returns. As completed documents come in, evaluators insert the (coded) responses into a computer, press a couple of keys, and wait for the tables and charts to roll out of the printer.

Convenient, neat, comparatively easy, and relatively inexpensive, the questionnaire has many advantages. Properly constructed, it can be a valuable source of data, especially when the evaluator has a large population or sample to analyze. Interviewing five hundred people would be a difficult and time-consuming task. Sending a questionnaire to that many people is not much more work than sending it to one hundred people.

The task of properly constructing a survey instrument is the most important part of the process. Good questionnaires can yield good data, but poor questionnaires produce unreliable data, a point that is frequently overlooked. Although it would be accurate to say that anyone can make up a questionnaire, considerable background and training are necessary if the data coming from that document are going to be useful. Anyone who has tried to construct a good questionnaire can testify that it is not a simple task.

A few sample questions from recent graduate student research projects illustrate some of the important characteristics of good questions.

a. *Isn't it true that people do not take drugs to feel better about themselves?* This question has several serious problems. First, the question is confusing because the writer has used a *double negative.* When respondents try to answer a double negative question, they are never sure what they are answering. As a result, the researcher gets unreliable data. (If respondents are not sure what the question is, researchers cannot be sure what they are analyzing!)

If a questionnaire has confusing questions, the researcher has to consider the responses unreliable. A double-negative question is the easiest illustration of a confusing question. But any experienced survey researcher can attest to the high number of respondents that get confused about various items. Ask people how often they attend church, and many of them will agonize about the meaning of the word "attend." "Does that mean staying for the whole service?" "If I go to the small chapel, does that count?" "Should I include those times when I went to my neighbor's church?"

"Do you enjoy your work?" might sound like a straightforward question, but only until the researcher discovers that half the sample defined "enjoy" in completely different ways, none of which the researcher intended. The other half was not sure what the researcher meant by the term "work." Confusing questions are easy to construct. Clarity is not as easy.

b. *How old are you?* This question seems clear, but here directness is a problem. To many people, being asked a question about their age (or income, or ethnic group) is too direct; it may also be embarrassing, or even irritating. They often ignore the question. Or they may simply lie about the answer.

This inclination to not tell the truth is why most questionnaires have "categories" for responses to these more sensitive questions like "How old are you?" Categories might be "21–35," "36–44," and so on. Giving respondents categories makes it easier for them to reveal characteristics such as age. And it is then more likely that evaluators will end up with reliable data!

Whenever researchers want answers to questions that respondents might regard as "too direct," they have to find a way of getting that information without sounding threatening. Accomplishing this is often difficult.

c. *A series of unusual sexual practices is listed below. Please make a check mark in front of each one of these practices that you have tried at some point in your life.* Though this question might be interesting to researchers, the phrasing ignores the potential sensitivity of the topic. Some people would not want to answer this type of question, however interesting it might be.

Whenever researchers want to obtain information that is potentially embarrassing to respondents, they have to consider the possibility that people may not respond, or if they respond, they will do so in a "socially acceptable" way.

With sensitive topics, it is necessary to look for ways to give individuals the ability to respond without "incriminating themselves." One way to accomplish this is to phrase the question in a way that the respondent feels comfortable in answering truthfully. For example, "Most people have engaged in the following sexual practices at some point in their lives. Which ones have you tried?"

Another common device is to assure the respondent of complete anonymity. This is often not easy, especially when the questionnaire is sent through the mail. But if individuals can feel assured that their replies are not going to be singled out for special attention or that they cannot be identified, they are more likely to respond to sensitive questions.

d. *Tell something about how religious you are.* Open-ended questions like this are good for generating new items of information, ones that the evaluators did not anticipate. Unfortunately, such questions also pose a problem because of their ambiguity. If people are not sure what the question wants from them, they are more than likely either to not answer it or to reply superficially.

It is also possible that different people will interpret this kind of question in different ways. One person might regard himself as religious because he goes to church every Christmas, rain or shine. Another individual, though she attends church every day of the year, might describe herself as "not very religious" because she firmly believes that once a day is not nearly enough.

The number of potential bad examples of questions is virtually endless. And though it is easy to look at these questions and criticize their wording, constructing a competent survey instrument is an extremely difficult, frustrating task. But if evaluators want to use this technique, they must learn to write questions.

The use of poorly constructed questions will generate unreliable data. Another problem is that even carefully reasoned questions can be confusing to respondents. This explains why it is essential to *pretest* survey instruments. Pretesting a questionnaire involves the distribution of a few, perhaps five or ten, questionnaires to selected individuals. In the Meals on Wheels Program, evaluators would distribute the questionnaire to this small number of meal recipients.

After these few people responded to the questionnaire, the evaluators would talk to them personally, getting their comments about whether the document was too long, if any questions were confusing, and whether they were completely honest in responding to all the questions. The results of this pretest would enable evaluators to judge the effectiveness of the various questionnaire items and to make any appropriate changes. Evaluators who do not pretest a questionnaire are asking for trouble.

Another important questionnaire technique is a "social desirability scale." Years ago, a comprehensive study of mental illness found that people indicated the presence of severe mental symptoms in their lives even though they had not actually experienced these conditions. It turned out that the respondents reported those symptoms because they assigned a high social value to them. If you did not have these signs of stress from your work, you were not sufficiently involved with your job. Or your job was not that important. Surprises like these in the data are always intriguing, but they can also produce headaches for researchers.

A social desirability scale on a questionnaire gives researchers a way to find out whether unusually high or low "social desirability" of items affects the responses to those items. The number of responses to a mailed questionnaire can also present some problems for researchers. Once the questionnaire goes out, whether it comes back completed is largely beyond the control of the evaluators. Questionnaire response rates of 30 to 40 percent are common enough for researchers to describe them as "average." Although that kind of average might be sufficient for a general survey, evaluators who rely on a 30 percent response rate from a sample are taking a substantial risk.

When 70 percent of the people do not respond to a questionnaire, this means that evaluators are working from data that exclude *seven out of every ten respondents*. The potential for significant distortion in those data is considerable. Unless evaluators resort to procedures such as follow-up reminder calls, low questionnaire response rates are to be expected.

Even a higher return rate is no guarantee of high quality survey data. When researchers mail out the instrument, or even after they hand it to respondents, they assume that the respondents (the addressees) will answer the questions. But there is no guarantee of that. The respondents could give the questionnaire to a neighbor or to one of their children. Maybe they filled it out but did it on the way to work, when they were thinking of other things.

If they wait until they get home after an especially long, frustrating day, they may decide to take out their irritations on the questionnaire. They respond to the questions about "that damn program" in a way that reflects their general mood more than their actual reactions to the program. These are the kinds of possibilities that researchers must consider, and they have to be part of the decision framework.

The length of a questionnaire is also an item worth mentioning. Though there are no absolute standards, evaluators should remember that questionnaires are an imposition on people's lives. Few people "love" to fill out questionnaires.

It is one thing to send a questionnaire that requires only a few minutes to complete; not many people object to that commitment. It is another demand entirely to send a lengthy document needing several hours of concentrated thought. Researchers should not be surprised that so few of those lengthy questionnaires are returned.

As with any research technique, the questionnaire has unique strengths and special weaknesses. Some researchers consider it an invaluable tool. Others refuse to use a questionnaire unless there are no alternatives. In some situations, such as those cases where personal contact with the program participants is impossible, a questionnaire might end up being the technique of last resort.

The best advice is, if you are using a questionnaire, use a good one. If the questionnaire is good and the sample is representative, the data-gathering process can produce useful information.

Interviews

An interview is a research technique, but it is also a personal encounter. With this technique, the evaluators talk individually with program participants to get the information firsthand. In the hands of a skilled researcher, the personal interview can be one of the best "open-ended" techniques available. The interviewer can go anywhere the discussion takes him. This capacity for exploration allows new and potentially valuable information to appear that would otherwise not have been revealed.

One reason interviews are not used more often is partly due to the absence of skilled interviewers. Acquiring interviewing skills takes time, along with experience.

Evaluators cannot afford many poor interviews. A poorly trained interviewer can cause a catastrophe. The researchers are talking to program participants, employees, and a variety of other people involved in the program. With a poorly chosen remark, a casual repeating of an overheard comment, or a hasty generalization, an interviewer can cause all sorts of problems for the program and the evaluation.

There are not many specific interviewing skills, but the ones that do exist are vital. One skill is the ability to talk to people and, in the process, to give the impression of interest, sincerity, and a high degree of professionalism. During the interview, sensitive topics are often discussed. If the interviewer does not know how to handle those topics, or if he or she projects a feeling of insincerity in those encounters, the results could be disastrous.

Good interviewing requires an ability to relate to other people. Some people do not have this ability, but this is not necessarily a fatal weakness. If an evaluator lacks that skill, she or he can and should rely on someone else to conduct the interviews.

The interviewer also needs to have "listening skills." Listening skills are the techniques used to let the respondents know that the interviewer is listening to what they are saying.

The primary purpose of an interview during a program evaluation is to get information from the people interviewed. A wealth of information can come from these sessions, but only as long as the interviewer is listening and not talking. "You can't learn anything while you are talking" is a good adage for the interviewer to remember. Listening techniques are also used to keep the respondent talking.

Silence is an effective listening technique. Most people do not like a conversational vacuum, so if the evaluator is able to keep silent, the respondent will usually continue talking. After asking a good leading question, the interviewer need only sit there, wait, and listen.

Another productive listening technique is "neutral comments." These short utterances tell the respondent that the interviewer is still listening and wants to hear more. The interviewer can accomplish those assurances without expressing any support or disapproval of what the respondent has been saying.

Whatever methods the interviewer uses, listening techniques place the interviewing emphasis where it should be—on the respondent. Evaluators who plan to conduct interviews should work on these skills.

Another important interviewing technique involves the ability to pursue a particular topic or issue until enough information has been obtained. This "probing" technique is necessary whenever the interviewer has reason to suspect that the whole truth has not emerged (which is most of the time!). An interviewer who accepts whatever respondents say without challenge might as well use mailed questionnaires. It would save time.

The advantage of interviewing is the face-to-face encounter and the opportunities it provides for getting at the truth. Respondents often give easy or comfortable replies to questions from interviewers, especially when the questions concern sensitive topics. The interviewer has to challenge those comfortable or sterile replies if the resultant data are going to be worth the time and money.

Here is a transcript from one part of an interview with an individual who completed a job training program.

INT.: Please tell me about the circumstances in your leaving the job you obtained after graduating from the training program.
RES.: It wasn't enough of a challenge.
INT.: Challenge?
RES.: Well, I wanted something with more of a challenge.
INT.: What do you mean by challenge?
RES.: You know, a challenge in the job. Something different, you know.
INT.: Mr. _____ , everyone says they want a job with more challenge, and I don't know exactly what that means. Tell me specifically what you did not like about the job in the pet cemetery.
(silence)
RES.: I just didn't like it. It wasn't me.
INT.: You mean you were willing to give up a regular job when you have bills to pay simply because the job wasn't you? That doesn't make much sense, does it?

Toward the end of this exchange, the interviewer is obviously pressing the respondent to the point of being rude. Rudeness, though, is not the interviewer's intention. He is conducting these interviews to obtain accurate information. The interviewer does not want unreliable information. If he writes down the first thing said by the respondent, he would have nothing more than a series of vague replies. Analyzing vague replies would be difficult.

Vague, incomplete, or inconsistent answers do not produce useful analyses. Evaluators need details from their interviews. Interviewers have to probe vague or noncommittal replies until those details emerge. (Or until the respondent asks the evaluator to leave!)

New interviewers frequently ask about the desirability of using audio or video taping equipment during an interview. This is another issue where opinion varies. Recording a conversation without the interviewee's consent is unethical and sometimes illegal. If the interviewee consents to being recorded, the interview should take place in full view of any recording equipment. That equipment can be disconcerting to the interviewee. If he is uncomfortable, the interview is ultimately less productive.

A surprising problem that arises when recording equipment is used is its effect on the interviewer. When researchers use recording equipment, they often rely on the device to do their listening. The result can be a perfect transcription of a poor interview.

Time is another consideration and a resource the evaluator should have in abundance if interviews are the chosen technique. Interviews take a considerable amount of time. A standard interview, even one with only a few questions, can easily last for an hour. Even this allows only a few moments for pleasantries at both the beginning and end of the interview. Those pleasantries are essential, not incidental.

After the formal interview is completed, the interviewer has to transcribe those hastily written interview notes into a verbatim narrative (or as close to it as possible). Then the researcher must convert these raw data into the categories he or she will eventually analyze.

The time needed for all these procedures is considerable. If evaluators are interviewing a large sample, then a considerable expense of time and money is inevitable.

In summary, if evaluators elect to use interviews as part of the data-gathering scheme, they should be sure that the people who do the interviewing have the skills and the training to do them well. There are no advantages from poor interviews. On balance, interviews are probably one of the best data-gathering techniques for program evaluations. Properly done, interviews can produce data that will allow the evaluators to develop a productive and insightful assessment. But these advantages come at a considerable cost of time and money. That cost factor will have to be assessed as part of the decision process.

Participant Observation

If evaluators decide to use the participant observer technique to gather some of the program information, they have to get personally involved in on-going social situations. With this technique, the researchers participate in the various activities or whatever else is going on in the program they are evaluating.

In the Meals on Wheels Program, the evaluators would probably ride along with the drivers, perhaps even delivering a few meals. They would spend time talking with the meal recipients. It would be within reason if they brought along meals for themselves and shared the meal hour with recipients.

The researchers would be interested in anything and everything that is happening with the program. They would watch and listen to everything from staff meetings to meal planning. When they are finished, they would know the program thoroughly and from personal experience. This individual experience is the primary advantage of a technique that is quite demanding in terms of time.

Participant observation is a considerable departure from the other major forms of data gathering. The evaluators are not asking a series of questions, although they may throw in some "short" questions during these personal encounters. And they are not passing out questionnaires, although this, too, can be part of participant observation. What the evaluators are doing is watching and recording virtually everything that takes place, from where people are sitting to what they are saying. It is research in a very personal and intense way.

This technique requires a lot of time. It will even take time to establish the reason for the evaluators' presence at the site. They cannot simply show up and start taking notes. The quality of observational data rests on the assumption that a researcher sees what really takes place. The presumption of that quality is more reasonable when the researcher has become "part of the scenery." That kind of familiarity does not surface in only one or two appearances.

As a result, a good deal of the time spent doing the observing will be "unproductive." Researchers are going to spend time doing things or perhaps talking to people that have little direct relationship to the specific goals of the evaluation. Even if the relationship is indirect or nonexistent, there is no way around this additional time investment.

There is always some "dead time" in the participant observation process, and researchers have to be prepared to invest it.

Transcribing field notes means more hours at the desk. After the transcription, when the field notes become a working narrative of the researcher's experiences and impressions, someone has to bring those data together so that the information necessary for the evaluation can be extracted. Analysis time for participant observation data can also be lengthy.

The advantage of the participant observation technique is that it provides details about a program that would (probably) not be otherwise available to evaluators. These details emerge because they are recorded by the professional researcher and not by a third party.

If time is limited, the participant observation technique may be used for only a part of the entire project. Researchers can go into the field for a few weeks rather than for several months. To provide evaluators with a firsthand, unscreened version of a program, the participant observer technique has no equal.

There is one disadvantage with participant observation that should be mentioned. After spending considerable time with the individuals in the program, researchers often become emotionally attached to the people they are studying. Researchers often spend eight hours a day studying a program and the people involved in it. It is not surprising that they get to know and like many people. Employees, program participants, site managers — evaluators meet these people daily. They eat with them, work with them, and laugh with them. Later, they are supposed to return to their office, record what these people said and did, and then analyze those data as though they had no knowledge of the personalities involved. This is not easy, and on occasion, it becomes impossible.

The tendency for researchers to become over-involved with their subjects is called "going native." The inclination to go native is understandable, but it cannot be allowed to affect the program evaluation. If strong feelings emerge, the evaluator needs to recognize the situation and deal with it.

The best insurance against having these feelings affect the analysis is for the evaluator to collect enough data from other sources so that subjective judgments do not overshadow objective facts. Another form of insurance is for the researcher to rely on the assessments of those who have not gathered participant data.

Even with these potentially significant limitations, though, participant observation is a valuable technique. If the time and the money are available, the evaluator has the opportunity for some unique insights when this technique is utilized.

Official Publications

Official publications, or "documents," is a broad category of information sources. It includes all those materials waiting for evaluators who know where to look and how to look. The "where" is usually the easiest part. The "how" can be more difficult.

The federal government is one of the primary sources of these documents. This level of government is a major producer of reports and statistics that evaluators might want to use. The number of federal publications will stagger the mind of a researcher who is exploring this resource for the first time. The Census Department's publications alone provide stacks of statistical data on a variety of topics. These data in particular are frequently useful in program evaluations. The primary limitation with census figures is that they are frequently not up to date.

State and local governments also publish statistics regularly. Evaluators should also consider looking at the many reports and publications issued by private organizations such as annual reports and internal memoranda.

The primary advantage of these documents is that they already exist and thus there are few, if any, costs associated with using them. The information is right there, printed and ready to use. Evaluators need only obtain a copy.

This ready availability should not obscure some of the potential problems with using these various documents. The primary problem is that the information in those professional-looking documents might not be accurate. The Uniform Crime Reports put out by the F.B.I. is a good example. The UCR looks precise, and some researchers are inclined to accept their numbers uncritically. That is usually a mistake. The F.B.I. only compiles and publishes these data. They are not involved in the actual data gathering. When they publish the UCR, the Bureau uses figures submitted by police departments and agencies around the country. Thus, the UCR is only as good as the reporting of the individual police departments. The accuracy of that reporting has, on more than one occasion, been less than credible. Anyone who uses the Uniform Crime Reports has to confront the credibility not of the F.B.I. but of each local police department that submits those reports.

Several years ago, I was involved in a research project that relied on a federal government publication called *Vital Statistics of the United States* as a source for mortality data. This publication is a comprehensive document, with detailed charts and official figures that provide information on mortality patterns throughout the country.

During the course of that research, I made hospital rounds with a physician. The doctor stopped by the nurses' station to sign some documents. When I asked him what he was signing, the doctor replied, "Death certificates." I asked him what he used as the explanation for the cause of death, since he was not looking at the patient charts and obviously had no intention of looking at the bodies. The physician replied, "I put down anything that the coroner won't send back. These forms are a pain, anyway."

The doctor was probably right. Pain or not, though, those death certificates provide the raw material for the *Vital Statistics* publication. It made me realize that the tables in that publication were not nearly as impressive as they once appeared.

The point here is not that evaluators should ignore official documents or statistics. Quite the contrary. These stacks of information are widely available, and evaluators would be foolish not to use them. But it is important to be cautious when using material collected by someone else.

The first thing researchers should do before relying on the information from official documents, no matter how "authoritative" they appear to be, is to determine the primary source of that information. Even if the source is suspect, researchers may decide to use the documents. But in such cases, they can insert a higher degree of caution into the analysis.

On the other hand, if researchers can corroborate the official information with data from another source, they can use those statistics with greater confidence. Either way, it pays to check the information and its sources carefully.

Another problem with data from published sources is that they may exist in a form that evaluators do not want or need. Data on crime statistics, for example, might be broken down by city and county, when evaluators need the information by individual neighborhood.

In evaluating the meals program, for example, the researchers want demographic information broken down into the areas served by the various program sites. There is little likelihood that they could obtain census information in that form. "What you see is what you get" is the situation encountered by most researchers when they rely on official statistics. And if what they get is not what they need, they are usually out of luck.

Official documents can be valuable resources for evalutors. But they have their limitations and weaknesses. As with other techniques, it is necessary to weigh the advantages against the disadvantages.

Unobtrusive Measures

On occasion, evaluators may want to gather information without making direct contact with program participants. The program under review might involve individuals who would be sensitive to direct queries. Prison parolees are one example of this type of population. People recovering from drug abuse are another.

The procedures for obtaining information in an indirect fashion are called "unobtrusive measures." With these techniques, the research is described as unobtrusive because the individuals studied presumably have no idea someone is looking at their actions.

For example, if an evaluator decides that it would be difficult to get truthful answers from recovering alcoholics about their consumption patterns, she may decide that the only valid way to assess the effectiveness of the treatment program is to go through the home garbage of the program participants. Or she might decide to sit in neighborhood bars, watching and listening. She could also browse retail liquor outlets to check on individual purchasing patterns.

The advantage of unobtrusive measures, the absence of any direct contact with respondents, is that the evaluator does not have to worry about incorrect information (lying) or effects caused by the researcher's presence. But the research *could* yield misleading information.

Misleading information is a problem with this type of technique because the researcher may not have any idea that the information is incorrect. The researcher could have found many whiskey and wine bottles in garbage bags, and those bottles could be seen as evidence of a continued high level of alcohol consumption. But empty bottles might also be the results of a wedding party for a member of the family. The program participant may have consumed only tonic water!

Unfortunately, the evaluator has no way of knowing about the tonic water if she relies solely on unobtrusive techniques. This weakness is a good argument for using unobtrusive measures in connection with another data-gathering technique.

This category of research techniques fosters considerable creativity. It is hard to come up with a way of gathering information that does not involve people contact, so when a researcher does find a way, it is usually creative.

A student in a university research class wanted to measure the level of "honesty" in the American population. Not satisfied with existing measures, she decided to use an unobtrusive measure. She addressed forty envelopes to herself and scattered the (coded) envelopes around the downtown metropolitan areas. If an envelope was mailed back to her, she counted that location, and that individual, as "honest."

The researcher provided a temptation for these respondents. It did not require much scrutiny to see that there was cash in the envelopes. Actually, what appeared to be cash was play money that looked like the real thing. If an individual opened the envelope, he or she found a short letter explaining the study and a form asking the finder to explain the reasons he or she opened the envelope. There was another pre-addressed, stamped envelope that the respondent could use to mail the reply. Obviously, if the explanations indicated an interest in the money, or if the envelope never came back, the response area was considered "dishonest."

The project produced a number of interesting experiences. One individual who found an envelope drove clear across the city to personally deliver it to the student. "I knew there was money inside, and I didn't want to take any chances on the mail," he told her. The student felt good about the incident, but she also regretted that the man drove so far to deliver play money. Understandably, she elected not to tell him that the whole thing was a research experiment.

Unobtrusive techniques can also produce ethically questionable procedures. The U.S. Supreme Court has ruled that once garbage is on the street, it belongs to the public at large. But not everyone shares that legal opinion. At the very least, people can be expected to be upset when someone opens their plastic garbage bags.

Although unobtrusive measures can be creative and productive ways to generate "uncontaminated" data, they can also be a way of getting information that will lead evaluators in unproductive directions. The key, as with other techniques, is that researchers must know what they are doing.

Other research techniques are available to evaluators, but we have covered the ones used most often in program evaluations. The important thing for evaluators to remember is that there are a variety of techniques from which to select. If a situation requires something different in a data-gathering device, evaluators should consider whatever might be appropriate under the circumstances. Projective techniques, experiments, even computer simulations are other research tools. Used properly, they may all be of help. With data-collection, as with measurement and design selection, evaluators must spend whatever time is available and necessary to do the job properly.

A powerful design, sound measurement, and effective data-gathering should help to produce a strong and effective program evaluation. They should also contribute to another important element in the evaluation—the analysis of the data. That important topic is the subject of the next chapter.

Selected Readings

Campbell, D. T., and Stanley, J. C. (1963). "Experimental and Quasi-Experimental Designs for Research on Teaching." In N. L. Gage, ed., *Handbook of Research on Teaching.* Chicago: Rand McNally.

This article has a comprehensive listing and explanations of the relative strengths and advantages of various research designs.

Fear, R. A. (1958). *The Evaluation Interview: Predicting Job Performance in Business and Industry.* New York: McGraw-Hill.

Though written for individuals who are hiring new employees, this book has many useful suggestions about the techniques of interviewing.

Goffman, E. (1961). *Asylums.* New York: Anchor Books.

A fascinating and readable narrative about life in a mental institution, and an illustration of the kind of information that can come from the use of participant observation.

Gordon, R. L. (1975). *Interviewing: Strategy, Techniques, and Tactics.* Homewood, IL: Dorsey Press.

A comprehensive book. It goes into everything from the ethics of interviewing to the process of selecting appropriate interviewers.

Katzer, J., Cook, K. H., and Crouch, W. W. (1991). *Evaluating Information: A Guide for the Uses of Social Science Research.* New York: McGraw-Hill.

This book provides a good overview of how knowledge is obtained. It has a light, readable style and, not incidentally, a good chapter on statistical analysis.

McCall, G., and Simmons, J. L., eds. (1969). *Issues in Participant Observation: A Text and Reader.* Reading, PA: Addison-Wesley.

Still the best general introduction to the technique of participant observation.

Miller, D. C. (1983). *Handbook of Research Design and Social Measurement.* New York: Longman.

Among a variety of good source books for social measurements, this is one of the best.

Oppenheim, A. N. (1966). *Questionnaire Design and Attitude Measurement.* New York: Basic Books.

An excellent resource for those interested in the techniques of questionnaire construction.

Phillips, D. L. (1971). *Knowledge from What? Theories and Methods in Social Research*. Chicago: Rand McNally.

The author criticizes what he terms "sterile, unproductive, unimaginative investigations."

Sonquist, J. A., and Dunkelberg, W. C. (1977). *Survey and Opinion Research: Procedures for Processing and Analysis*. Englewood Cliffs, NJ: Prentice-Hall.

A detailed look at the survey technique. The authors even discuss how to negotiate with people in the computer lab.

CHAPTER FOUR

Organizing Evaluation Data

"Is this chapter going to be about statistics?" The answer is both yes and no. Good news and bad news! Although this chapter focuses on statistics and the role these procedures have in the evaluation process, there is not enough space in one small chapter to go into much detail. This necessarily limited treatment should minimize everyone's discomfort.

The pervasive fear about statistics is evident in classrooms and elsewhere. But numbers are not going to go away even if people dislike dealing with them. The question is not whether to deal with statistics, but whether we deal with them intelligently. But how does one get people to confront numbers? Put these numbers in front of otherwise open-minded people and their eyes glaze over. They begin searching for a way either to change the subject or to leave the room. "I've just never been good with numbers," they insist. And they may be right. They never have been any good with numbers, although the reasons for this has less to do with ability than with bad experiences. It is worth noting how often negative perceptions about numbers began with a bad experience in elementary school.

Evaluators do not have the luxury of ignoring numbers. Numerical analysis (statistics, in other words) is an integral part of the evaluation process. Evaluators cannot avoid these procedures unless they want to put themselves at the mercy of others.

Statistical analysis is not as bad as some people think it is. It does involve some math, but the procedures used in statistics are mostly elementary: addition, subtraction, multiplication, division, some square roots, and a little algebra. If you can deal with these procedures, you should have no problem with statistical computations.

Problems or not, there are no alternatives to using some statistics in the evaluation process. If the Meals on Wheels Program evaluators were statistics-shy and they wanted to publish the evaluation data without using statistical procedures, they would put out a thousand-page report. Most of those dreary pages would be a case-by-case listing of the individual responses to the various questions. It is hard to imagine how tedious a document like that would be for readers.

Without statistics, the evaluation report would have to list each separate item on the program questionnaire. Then, for each question, there would be the details from several hundred individual responses.

The verbatim transcripts for the interviews would come next, page after page of quotes without summaries or even an occasional graph. If the evaluators collected any participant observation data, those recorded details would also be listed on a day-by-day basis. It would be as exciting as reading the telephone book.

When people complain about understanding statistics, they are usually thinking about the data analyses that appear in textbooks and scholarly journals. The statistics used in these settings frequently are difficult for the nonpractitioner to understand. Even professionals may have trouble figuring out what those manipulations mean.

But instead of worrying about those more esoteric types of analysis, think about other forms of numerical analysis encountered every day. Newspapers regularly publish sports statistics. When was the last time readers complained that they did not understand batting averages, serve velocity, or yards per carry in a third down and short situation? The financial pages always have a variety of indices with charts and graphs that show yearly and monthly trends of markets and individual stocks. Price/earnings ratios, rates of return, Dow-Jones averages — even casual investors seem to be able to follow the manipulation of these numbers. There never seems to be a clamor for "simpler statistics" from the stock market!

And every American taxpayer knows enough statistics to get angry when the government talks about a 10 percent tax increase or a jump in some surtax! These and countless other examples illustrate the considerable range of statistical information present in our lives. Most Americans deal with numbers regularly, whether they want to or not.

"But I'm not talking about pie charts, tax increases, or batting averages. I'm talking about those things with the formulas and arrows pointing in all directions. I don't understand those things," you might say. Maybe no one understands "those things." But that is another issue. The statistical procedures done for most evaluations are usually far easier to understand.

Statistics in evaluation research have two basic functions: to analyze the data and to serve as a form of communication between evaluators and audience. These two functions are related, and the closeness of that relationship should be the cornerstone for any statistical analysis evaluators elect to do.

A primary function of statistics is to analyze the data. Evaluation statistics organize and summarize the data so that they tell a story. Statistics describe data in a way that is different from what a novelist tries to do, but different only in style. Both the researcher and the novelist are describing a set of events; one uses numbers and the other relies on words. They both want their readers to visualize, and understand, what they are saying.

If the background data from the meals program show that the participants have an average tenth-grade education, their median family income is $11,500 per year, and 42 percent of them live in substandard housing, readers of that report would have some idea of the conditions and lives of those individuals. Although John Steinbeck's description of poverty in *The Grapes of Wrath* would be more graphic, numbers can be an effective way of raising images in the reader's mind.

Organizing, communicating, and raising images are the goals of statistical analysis. Statistics are not sterile and meaningless numbers. They are an indispensable aid for the evaluator who has to tell a detailed story about a complex social program.

Another element in statistical analysis that seems to bother people is the use of symbols. The various symbols seem, at first, glance, to be meaningless, but if people would see those signs for what they are, a form of shorthand, much of that confusion would disappear. Those various symbols are a shorter, more convenient, and presumably more effective way of describing procedures. In many respects, they are similar to traffic signals and road signs.

It is hard to imagine a road sign that said "There is a dangerous curve ahead so slow down." Who has time to read all those words? Everyone knows that a curved arrow is the sign for a curve in the road. That symbol isn't confusing. It makes sense. And so do the symbols in statistics, once you get used to them.

Writing out "add up all the figures in the column and then divide by the total number of those figures" is a cumbersome and confusing way to describe what needs to be done. It is much easier to write:

$$\Sigma x / f$$

This formula is the one for computing the arithmetic mean (an average). Rather than looking at this formula as a collection of confusing symbols, see it as shorthand. The "x" is simply a substitute for the words "the numbers in the column." The line "/" is a substitute for the statement "divide the top number by the bottom number." "Σ" means "the sum of," and "f" refers to the number of observations. When looked at like road signs, these symbols are less intimidating. The arrows, lines, and letters are a way of telling readers what they have to do to compute the answer. Even the more complex formulae involve doing simple arithmetic procedures one step at a time.

The important task of this chapter is to illustrate the major statistical approaches used in evaluation research. This overview of descriptive and inferential statistics should provide you with an understanding of how each of these basic divisions of statistics functions and how each can contribute to a program evaluation. This statistical overview will be necessarily quick.

Numbers are the building blocks of the final evaluation. Even if the evaluators choose not to move those blocks around themselves, they should understand the way their associates are stacking them. Using statistics properly, evaluators have a new language at their command. With numbers, they can summarize the information that was gathered, analyze it, draw inferences from it, and then present the results in a way that is clear and understandable, even to all those people who are still avoiding numbers.

Descriptive Statistics

Descriptive statistics have a clear, easily understandable function. They describe a set of data. No mystery! These statistics provide the means for summarizing and conveying the characteristics of large bodies of information.

Descriptive statistics for groups are no different in principle from the descriptions of individuals. Describing a woman as being five feet, ten inches tall, weighing 142 pounds, and having dark curly hair tells us something about one person. Describing a group of people as averaging five feet, two inches in height and 155 pounds tells us something about the group's physical characteristics.

Using group descriptions is more efficient than individual descriptions, especially when there are many cases. One obvious limitation in using summaries, though, is that the reader loses considerable detail about those individuals. We may know the average weight of the group, but what about that one woman? What happened to her statistic?

Obviously, her number is not lost. Information on this woman and the rest of the individuals is now part of the group's data. The loss of individual details is one cost of using group descriptions. "Cost" may not be the most appropriate way to describe this difference, because evaluators rarely need details about individuals. They are interested in group patterns.

Were the characteristics of the control group similar to those of the experimental group? What happened to the experimental group's attitudes after they had been in the program for several years? Did the control group's level of psychological well-being also increase?

These questions are typical of the kind asked by evaluators as they search for the program's effects. The researchers are not usually interested in individual performances. Since details concerning individuals are generally not necessary, their loss is not important. If it is desirable to use information from individual cases, perhaps as anecdotal illustrations, those data are usually available.

The most commonly used descriptive statistic is probably the "average." It is commonly used but not always completely understood, as the following example illustrates.

One item the evaluators in the Meals on Wheels Program might want to look at is employee attitudes. The people working in that program play a vital role in its success. Understandably, the evaluators are interested in how the employees in the organization feel about their jobs.

Salary is an important ingredient in those jobs, so the evaluators are interested in these figures. They are especially curious about the salaries paid to the social workers. These people conduct the initial entry interviews with the program participants and their families, so they are especially important in setting the tone of the program.

The evaluators make an appointment with the program director to explain their interest in employee attitudes. "Since salaries are influential in these attitudes," they explain to the director, "it would help if you would provide us with a listing for last year's social worker salaries. Since we will be using averages in the report, no confidences will be broken."

The director is pleasant, but he shakes his head. "It is not really a problem," he says, "but I still can't release individual salary figures. Will it be acceptable if I give you the average social worker salary for last year rather than personal salaries?"

"Certainly," the evaluators reply. "After all, we were going to compute the average salary anyway. This would save us a few minutes of work."

The evaluators wait while the director slides his chair over to his computer and punches up some numbers. After a few minutes of work on the keyboard, he scribbles on a piece of paper and hands it to the group. The paper shows: "Average Social Worker salary, 1994: $30,625."

They thank him and go back to their office. "Not a bad income" one researcher says after they sit around a table to discuss some points in their ongoing analysis. "This is a good salary for the social workers in this program, especially considering that most of these people were hired right out of college." Every evaluator agrees that salaries should not be the main problem if employee attitudes turn out negative.

In an interview later that day, a case worker mentions unhappiness with her salary. She asks whether the evaluator agrees that she has reason to be dissatisfied. "Don't you think we are underpaid?" she asks.

The researcher shakes his head. "Well, it is not my position to agree or disagree with your feelings about your salary. Since you asked though, based on the figures I have, you and your colleagues are doing very well, especially in comparison with social workers in similar organizations."

She gives him a strange look, but says nothing else about the matter. An hour later, the same social worker comes to the evaluator's office and hands him a sheet of paper:

Salaries: Metropolis Senior Meals Program

Site Director	$90,000
Assistant Director	55,000
Director of Volunteers	25,000
Secretary	15,000
Social Work Counselors (5 @ $12,000)	60,000
Total Salaries	$245,000
Average Salary	$30,625

"Wait a minute," the evaluator says to his colleagues after the social worker leaves. "The figure the administrator gave us was not the average salary. That guy lied to us."

No he didn't. The formula the director used for that salary figure he gave to the evaluators was not for *the* average but for *an* average (i.e., the arithmetic mean). The mathematical process the director used was correct; the total salaries ($245,000) were divided by the number

79

of employees (8). The result of $30,625 may not be the *best* or even the most representative average. But it is *an average*.

The director did not lie to the evaluators. He may have misled them, and this misleading may or may not have been intentional. But he definitely did not lie to them. His "mistake," if that is what it can be termed, was in using an "inappropriate" statistic for the data.

After looking at the distribution of salaries, he should have used a descriptive statistic that accurately portrayed a "skewed" data set (clustered at one end of the distribution). In skewed data sets, an arithmetic mean average will produce a misleading interpretation.

An alternative average to use with skewed data is the "modal average" (the figure occurring the most frequently). The modal average salary here would be $12,000. That amount is still not a perfect fit for the data, but it is a better descriptive figure here than the arithmetic mean.

Descriptive statistics are supposed to describe the data accurately. If they do not, or if the story told is incomplete or misleading, then those statistics are not doing the job. In every case, the evaluators must use the most appropriate numerical analysis.

Even in cases where intentional deception is not involved, if individuals do not understand the statistic they are using, the results can be very misleading. Ignorance of statistical procedures can be as much a problem as perception. At least with intentional deception, the individual knows what he is doing.

Evaluators have to use descriptive statistics that accurately summarize the information without any misrepresentation of the general pattern in the data. Guarding against the potential for misrepresentation is often more difficult than it might seem. The following case illustrates how another type of misrepresentation can occur.

After a one-year intensive program designed to improve student spelling, the students at an elementary school took a national spelling test. The results were given to every student's family:

Below grade level:	9%
At grade level:	62%
Above grade level:	29%

At first glance, everyone involved with this spelling program was satisfied. After all, less than 10 percent of the school's students had spelling skills below grade level. So everyone should feel good about those scores. Although there was no information given on the methods of research used, the data here looked convincing.

The problem with these statistics is that the data are grouped into categories. "At grade level" and "below grade level" are reasonable categories, but evaluators should provide details about the composition of and distributions within any category used.

Those appealing test results may not be nearly as good as they look. Sixty-two percent of the students tested "at grade level." But how close were these students to their respective grade levels? It is conceivable that most of the students were within one or two points of being "below" their grade levels. A small change of two or three points in scores or in the definitions of the categories would mean that the proportion of students performing "at grade level" would drop dramatically. Similarly, nearly all of the students showing "above grade level" scores might be within two points of their grade levels. With the normal variations in objective testing, those students are as likely to be "at grade level" as they are to be above it.

By making a few changes in the definitions of the various categories—not arbitrary changes but ones based on the distribution of the student scores—evaluators would have an entirely different chart. Although not as positive or appealing to the program's administrators, the following would be a more accurate reflection of the data:

Below grade level:	39%
At grade level:	59%
Above grade level:	2%

The results of the spelling improvement program do not look nearly as good now, yet the data are the same. The only thing that changed was the format for categorizing the information. Though it would be possible to make a plausible argument for either of the two charts, "arguing" is not what evaluators should be doing.

Their job is to present the information in as accurate and as representative a fashion as possible. If it is appropriate to use categories to summarize the data, those categories should represent the most reasonable groupings. If responsible individuals or organizations, such as the federal government, dictate the use of specific categories, the evaluators' responsibility is not to criticize those groupings. But they still want to convey the information accurately. In a case like this, they would point out the potential problems with categories, discuss the range of student scores within each category, and then, perhaps, construct an alternate table so that the audience will have other ways of looking at the information. The evaluators' role is to present the information accurately and not to attempt to lead the audience in one particular direction.

Several charts and tables appear in this chapter, and these visual devices are another important descriptive statistic. Tables and charts are a means of organizing and displaying information. They are not statistical procedures, yet they are commonly considered a distinct area within descriptive statistics.

Tables and charts can be an effective means of conveying information *if* they are properly prepared. People often consider tables to be complicated, but they should not be a problem to read or interpret. When properly constructed, tables should be easy to understand.

Three simple rules govern table construction:

1. *Table titles should be complete,* and they should be descriptive. The title should tell the reader exactly what is in the table.
2. *Tables should be self-contained.* If readers look only at the table, they should have all the information they need. Readers of evaluation reports often turn to a table to check an interpretation or perhaps because they want to look at data patterns for themselves. Tables should provide enough information so that anyone can read them without looking for information or clarification within the written text. The information in the table includes categories used, column and row headings, sample size, and an explanation of "missing cases."
3. *Tables should be easy to read.* Tables and charts are visual aids and communication devices. They are not communication aids if readers get no message from them. It would be fair to say that if most of the reading audience is confused about the information in a table, the problem may lie with the table rather than with the audience.

Table readability is enhanced by simplicity. That simplicity is created by minimal categories, the lowest possible number of items, and a strong emphasis on aesthetics. The most popular tables have one, two, or three variables. An example of a one-variable table is shown in table 4.1. Most readers would have no problems interpreting the data on this one-variable table. The table follows the three basic rules of table construction; a clear title, self-contained, and easy to read. The title tells the reader exactly what is there. Readers can get what they need from the rest of the information provided within the table. If readers have questions about the evaluator's interpretations of these data, they can get the answers from the narrative.

A one-variable table should offer no significant obstacles for readers. The two-variable table is only slightly more complex. The data in table 4.2 are from a hypothetical prisoner early release program. This table also follows the basic rules: the title is complete and descriptive, the categories are clear, and the table is easy to read. The table includes two variables: the type of crime and the rate at which individuals were sent back to prison.

One point of potential dispute with the table involves the categories for one of the variables. The table lists various types of crime (i.e., violent, property, etc.), but it is not obvious what the researcher means by each category. What is included in "violent crime," for example? Does "drug offense" include both selling and using drugs? Some researchers argue that additional details like this should be part of any comprehensive table.

The extent of the information that should be provided in a table is a point of disagreement. The amount of information should make the table completely "self-contained," but on the other hand, the

Table 4.1 • *Family Income Distribution: Metropolis Meals on Wheels Program (N = 354)*

Income Level	Percentage
Low Income (under $15,000)	7%
Medium Income (15,000-39,999)	62%
High Income (40,000+)	31%
Total	100%

Source: Independent Survey, 1994.

Table 4.2 • *Success with Early Release from Prison, by Type of Crime (N = 744)*

	Percentage re-arrested within one year	
Individuals Jailed for:	yes	no
Violent crimes	32%	68%
Property crimes	18%	82%
Robbery/burglary	54%	46%
Drug offenses	41%	59%

83

possibilities for items to include are endless. Should the evaluator insert actual numbers as well as percentages? What about how the sample was drawn and whether the sample was randomized? Perhaps every column and row heading should be explained in detail!

Though there is no doubt that more information would produce a completely "self-contained" table, this benefit would come at the expense of the table's visual attractiveness as well as its overall comprehensiveness. There is a line where "self-contained" becomes confusion. If a table loses its communication function, the quality of being "self-contained" will be small consolation.

There is no easy answer here. An admittedly vague guideline is to put in enough information to answer the most pressing questions. Readers needing details on every item in the chart would have to consult the text. The alternative would be a cluttered table that would be of little value to anyone.

Visual clarity of the tables is important to evaluators, but so are the conclusions drawn from those tables. If evaluators put data into tables, they have to provide interpretations of those tables. Tables are not ornaments, something to be placed in a report and then forgotten. Tables are not always necessary, but if evaluators construct these visual devices, they need to use them in the narrative.

Finally, there are three-variable tables. The only difference between these tables and the other two kinds of tables is the introduction of one additional item, a third variable. One more variable does not sound like much. Occasionally, though, understanding the implications and the details in a three-variable table requires a few extra moments of study, even for the experienced reader.

Three-variable table 4.3 introduces "gender" into the earlier analysis of the relationship between type of crime and the success of an early release program. Although the use of three-variable tables can generate confusion, they may be necessary to convey a specific, important message. If three-variable tables are necessary, evaluators should take the time to guide readers through the interpretive stage.

Since the re-arrest rates for males and females are dramatically different in the three-variable tables, the evaluator should describe that difference. By referring to the information in the table and taking the discussion of the analysis step-by-step, even the least statistics-minded reader should be reasonably comfortable with the analysis and subsequent interpretations.

This brief overview of descriptive statistics has not been exhaustive. What it should have done is point out the potential value of statistics

Table 4.3 • *Success with Early Release from Prison*
(by sex and type of crime)

| | Males (N = 580) | | Females (N = 164) | |
| | Re-arrested within one year? | | Re-arrested within one year? | |
Type of crime	yes	no	yes	no
Violent crime	18%	82%	11%	89%
Property crime	43%	57%	18%	82%
Robbery/burglary	67%	33%	29%	71%
Drug offenses	62%	38%	21%	79%

in data management and illustrate the pitfalls that await those who are not familiar with these statistics.

Inferential statistics are not necessarily more complex, but they often provide more challenge for the researcher and the reader.

Inferential Statistics

Understanding inferential statistics requires a slightly different perspective, one more attuned to abstractions. Instead of *only* describing data, researchers use this *type* of statistical analysis to draw inferences. This distinction between describing and inferring is the reason for the additional complexities within this branch of statistics. The frustrations of those complexities disappear after researchers discover the value that comes from these procedures.

When doing social research, individuals seldom are able to learn the whole story. The incompleteness of the information might be caused by prohibitive costs, limitations in time, or the size of the population. Although researchers know only part (or a sample) of the story, they obviously want to go from what they already know to what they do not know. Making this move may sound unreasonable, but the use of inferential statistics makes this logical leap possible. And reasonable!

No magic is involved, no slight of hand or mirrors, only statistical procedures that allow us to make inferences about the unknown. Evaluation researchers should burn the term "possible" into their minds. These statistical procedures merely make inferences *possible*.

These procedures do not necessarily make inferences *correct,* and the distinction should be understood. The researcher is *inferring* from the known to the unknown. Even with the use of tested, standard procedures, those inferences are still *only inferences*. Inferential statements make a big jump, and evaluators have to remember that it is not always successful. The longer the jump, the greater the potential for a fall.

Wondering if the risk is worth it is usually a moot question. Inferential statistics are used because researchers either do not or cannot know the whole story. They have to get the whole story, or at least as close to it as possible, and the only means for achieving this proximity to the "whole truth" is to use statistical procedures.

The use of inferential statistics requires a grasp of "probability" because, in most of these cases, "certainty" does not exist.

"Probability" refers to the likelihood of an event occurring. If evaluators took a nationwide sample of high school students, for example, they could *never* be absolutely certain that the attitudes in the sample group reflected the distribution of the entire population. There is no way they could ever be sure, not unless they surveyed the nation's entire high school population. In this and in most other cases, then, there is no practical way to be certain about whether the sample reflects the general population. The comfort of "certainty" turns into the frustrations and doubts of "possibility." Were the attitudes reflected in the sample of high school students the same as would have been seen in a nationwide survey? Evaluators could provide data to show a 95 percent probability that they were the same. They could also show a 99 percent probability. But not 100 percent.

What are the chances of an individual drawing an ace from a deck of cards? People who play cards (with an honest deck) know that the chances are 4 in 52, or roughly an 8 percent chance. What are the chances of drawing to an inside straight? You need five cards in sequence to constitute a straight in poker: for example, 8-9-10-J-Q. If you hold four of these sequential cards and attempt to "fill it in" by drawing one of the middle cards, you are trying to "fill an inside straight." Here the odds or the probability become a little fuzzy because it is (usually) not possible to know exactly what cards your opponents have drawn. If you need a 10 to fill in a straight, the odds of drawing that 10 could be relatively good (if all four 10s are still in the deck). Or they could also be zero, if the player sitting across from you is holding four 10s. When poker players talk about percentages in drawing to an inside straight, they are basing their judgment on assumptions that may not be valid.

The notion of "questionable assumptions" is also important in understanding the nature of the probability used by evaluators. Very often, dubious assumptions play a role in calculating probability. For example, people say the probability of rain is 85 percent, the probability of a stock market drop is 60 percent, and the probability of a specific team winning the national championship is 40 percent. These assertions are based on past performances. If the stock market has dropped in six of the ten previous Januarys, it is within reason to talk about a "60 percent probability" of a January drop in the market. But that reliance on past performance makes the probability rate still questionable because there is no guarantee that current conditions are similar to those of earlier periods.

There is nothing wrong with using such figures, not as long as everyone realizes their tenuousness. They are based on the best available information. And that would be a reasonable way to describe inferential statistics — a means of making the best possible prediction from uncertain or incomplete information. It is, in other words, the best *guess* possible under the circumstances.

Describing inferences as "guesses" is not an argument against the use of these statistics. It is a word of caution, especially for evaluators. They must understand the limitations and the strengths of these procedures if they are to use them effectively and express the appropriate meaning to their audience.

Evaluators have to be careful about relying on these statistical procedures as the ultimate decision-making tool. Partly because of the apparent precision of statistics and partly because it is hard for anyone to argue with statistical procedures, evaluators are often tempted to rely on statistics to make the final decision about how well a program is doing. Using only statistical procedures to evaluate a program is generally not a good idea. Statistics in general, and inferential statistics in particular, can be an important tool, but they are not a substitute for an evaluator's own careful and critical thinking.

Inferential statistics rely on the notion of "statistical significance," another concept that is frequently misunderstood. We can use another example from the game of poker to illustrate the statistical significance.

Four people are playing the game of five card draw. In this game, every player draws five cards and has the option of exchanging, at most, three of those cards in the hopes of improving the betting quality of the hand. Bill is dealt four aces. Lucky Bill! That kind of hand occurs by chance about once in every three hundred thousand hands! In the next hand, Bill deals four aces to himself. The odds that the same card hand happened this second consecutive time by chance alone is roughly one in 73 billion hands. It is possible that mere chance gave Bill those two winning hands. But if a statistician had been in the game, he or she would have insisted that there was a "statistically significant" possibility that Bill's good fortune had nothing to do with mere chance.

No one (other than Bill) can be 100 percent sure that it *wasn't* luck that provided those cards to Bill. But the odds are against it. If I were sitting in that game, I would start watching Bill's sleeves. If he got four aces a third time that evening, Bill would have problems convincing me or anyone else of his honesty.

Statistical significance is a means of giving odds for or against the probability that something happened strictly by chance. Was it only by chance that Bill was dealt those winning hands, or was some other factor involved? The information available provides no way to be absolutely certain. Still, if someone had to place a bet, it would be a good idea to bet on the side of statistical significance. And the statistically significant odds are that Bill had something other than luck going for him.

With this basic understanding of probability and statistical significance, it is easier to see how evaluators might use inferential statistics in assessing a social project. As an example, suppose evaluators are directing the assessment of a new program changing a high school curriculum. These changes involve science subjects and a new method of teaching science to high school students.

There is not enough time or money to conduct a data-gathering process that would include every school. The evaluators decide to sample a group of ten schools. Five of these schools use the old curriculum (Group A), and five of the sample schools use the new curriculum (Group B). Students in each school took a ten-item science essay test, and researchers computed a total school average. The results were rounded to the nearest number. The scores for each of the ten schools are shown in figure 4.1.

Students from the schools that use the old curriculum (A) averaged 2.4 on the ten-item science test, and the students using the new curriculum averaged a score of 9. The question is, Was the 6.6 difference in scores large enough to conclude that students using the new curriculum learned significantly more than students using the old curriculum?

It is possible that the difference came from chance factors, that the scores are different because of things such as the day the tests were given or even the time of day. The same students might have different test scores on another day. The evaluators need to know if the difference between the two groups is statistically significant.

Even with a difference this large, there is no guarantee that all researchers would answer the question in the same way. If the difference

Figure 4.1 • *Scores on Science Tests from Groups Using Two Different Curricula*

Group A	Group B
3	8
2	10
4	9
1	10
2	8
$\Sigma = 12$	$\Sigma = 45$
$\overline{X} = 12/5 = 2.4$	$\overline{X} = 45/5 = 9$

had been smaller, the degree of potential dispute between researchers might be even greater. Some researchers would see a difference in averages of 3 as significant, while others would insist that a difference that small was due strictly to chance factors.

In any case, it is bad science and even worse social policy to rely on subjective judgments about the size of any difference. To test for the potential significance of the difference between the scores of these two groups, the evaluators could use a T-test, a statistic for testing the differences between two means taken from a small sample. There are usually several usable statistics that could apply in any given situation, and evaluators might want to consider looking at all of them.

In reviewing various statistical procedures, researchers look at the characteristics of the data before making a decision. A T-test, for example, requires that the data be "normally distributed" (i.e., equally distributed around the mean). This statistic also requires that the data be interval-level (i.e., the intervals are equidistant and thus can be added, subtracted, multiplied, or divided). The data here fit those requirements, so the T-test is as good as any other for helping with this assessment.

After solving the equation for the T-test, evaluators have a score of 9.71. They have gone from a difference in average scores of 6.6 to a T-score of 9.71. With a T-score, however, there is a little more to be done. Once the score has been calculated, the researcher consults a table of T-scores. The table shows that a difference this large (in the T-score) with a sample the size of this one would happen less than once in a hundred occurrences.

The testing difference between the two groups may have been due to time, day, or some other chance factors, but the odds are against it. That 6.6 figure is, in other words, a "statistically significant difference." The evaluators would probably conclude that the new curriculum was having a significant difference on how much the students were learning.

It is worth emphasizing that the conclusion about the differences in high school curricula *is not a certainty.* It is still possible — not likely, perhaps, but possible — that there is no difference in how much science students are learning from the two curricula. "*Probability* statistics" are not "*certainty* statistics." They provide researchers with a means of finding the most likely explanation, and "most likely" is as good as the explanations ever get.

It is also worth repeating that the decision about the effectiveness of the new curricula should not be decided *solely* on the basis of that single statistical test. A lot more information needs to go into the pot before any far-reaching decision like that is reached.

The now-familiar Meals on Wheels Program provides a means of looking at another frequently used inferential statistic. This statistic, the "Pearson product moment correlation coefficient," more commonly called "Pearson's r," is a way of examining relationships between variables.

The evaluators are testing for possible relationships between the income, educational level, and the psychological well-being of the meals program participants. The basic data assumptions of the Pearson's r statistic are ordinal-level data (data can be ranked from higher to lower), a normal distribution (distributed equally around the mean), and a linear relationship (when a change in y-value is accompanied by a corresponding change in x-value). Researchers believe that these assumptions about the data are reasonable. The data are fed into a computer, and the result is a correlation matrix (table 4.4). The evaluators used

Table 4.4 • *Pearson Correlations: Income, Education, and Psychological Well-Being (N = 341)*

	Education Level	Income	Well-being
Education level	1.000	.6823*	.0268
Income	.6823*	1.000	.8122*
Well-being	.0268	.8122*	1.000

Source: 1993 Independent Survey.

* = significant at .05 level

the .05 level of statistical significance here. This means that, if the relationships show a statistical significance, they could assume that ninety-five times out of a hundred, the patterns in these data happen only because of something other than chance factors.

The data here show statistically significant relationships between income and psychological well-being. This pattern might be important, but the evaluators have to remember that a demonstrated statistical significance is not *proof* of a relationship between those two things. It is only an indication that a relationship *might* exist between the two variables.

Evaluators who go from this correlation matrix to a conclusion that "income has a positive relationship with psychological well-being; higher income people will obviously always feel better about themselves" are asking for arguments. And they would get them as soon as someone who understands statistics reads that table.

With correlations, as with most other statistics, there are a few "peculiarities" that researchers should know. Even small correlations will be "statistically significant" with large sample sizes. With the sample used here, a correlation coefficient of "only" .1650 would show a statistical significance. That figure might be significant to a computer, but it would probably be of no interest to a program director.

That is another point worth some emphasis. In these days of computers, it is easy to turn the thought process over to the machine. Press the enter button and wait for the machine to figure out what is significant. The procedure is easy, but can become a problem if the computer produces decisions that make sense statistically but are "nonsense" otherwise. Evaluators should guard against relying on machine-induced thought.

In summary, the process of generating the data for a program evaluation is a time-consuming and often difficult process. But sometimes the subsequent analysis is just as difficult as the data-gathering, though in not the same way. Evaluators now have to organize the information in a way that exposes it to reasonable scrutiny. Evaluators do not necessarily have to be statisticians, but they should feel comfortable enough with numbers so that they can organize their data effectively.

Data analysis is an indispensable tool in the evaluation process. Using statistics is a part of this analysis. Despite their mystique, statistics are not panaceas; they are not substitutes for weaknesses in the methodological structure of the evaluation, and even the best statistical procedure will not compensate for a poor methodology. They are also not substitutes for clear thinking.

Yet statistics must be given their place. They are an essential ingredient in any program evaluation. With all their limitations, it would be a fatal mistake for any evaluator to allow a well-executed evaluation to disintegrate because of an inadequate or inappropriate analysis. Even a perfectly prepared evaluation can be swallowed up by an ineffectual analysis.

It might help if evaluators think of statistics as a verbal rather than a mathematical language. Working with prose might make it easier to compose the most insightful description possible of a program's activities.

Selected Readings

Anderson, T. R., and Zelditch, M. (1975). *A Basic Course in Statistics*. New York: Holt, Rinehart and Winston.
> This is an unusually readable primer in statistical analysis.

Blalock, H. M. (1972). *Social Statistics*. New York: McGraw-Hill.
> Although not an easy book to get through, this one has a wealth of information on various statistical procedures.

Cozby, P. (1984). *Using Computers in the Behavioral Sciences*. Palo Alto, CA: Mayfield.
> The book has a variety of useful sections on how computers can be used for statistical analyses.

Dewdney, A. K. (1992). *Two Hundred Percent of Nothing: How to Tell When Numbers Lie*. New York: Wiley.
> An entertaining look at the way numbers are used to mislead consumers.

Fox, W. (1992). *Social Statistics Using MicroCase*. Washington, DC: Microcase.
> An excellent blend of computer lore and learning statistics.

Hedderson, J. (1991). *SPSS/PCT Made Simple*. Belmont, CA: Wadsworth.
> A good handbook for users of SPSS (Statistical Program for the Social Sciences).

Hurlburt, R. T. (1994). *Comprehending Behavioral Statistics*. Pacific Grove, CA: Brooks/Cole.
> A handy and reliable statistics book for the novice.

McKeown, P. G. (1988). *Living with Computers*. New York: Harcourt Brace Jovanovich.
> Statistical analyses these days frequently require the use of computers. Even if not required, computers make the analysis far less time consuming than it would otherwise be. For the non–computer user, this book is an excellent introduction.

Is This Program Working?
Making the Vital Judgment

By now, it should be obvious that the evaluation process is a fairly logical procedure; getting the background information, laying out the program's goals, insuring adequate measurement of variables, conducting a thorough data-gathering process coupled with an effective evaluation design, and finally going through a careful analysis of the data. If evaluators work through these steps carefully, they have done their job — or most of it! Depending on the situation, the trickiest part of the evaluation may be still ahead. All of those columns of data have to be added up and combined, and that fundamental equation has to be solved. This is the point in the process where the evaluators throw everything into the pot in an attempt to answer that central question: What is this program accomplishing?

Problems for evaluators can arise even at this point. Although the information collected may have been excellent in every detail, evaluators may interpret those assembled "facts" in different ways. Despite the volumes of material on hand, evaluators still have questions to resolve and issues to settle. It is not yet time to relax!

The most basic question to be answered now is whether the program has been effective. It is possible that the answer is obvious, and if so, there is no analysis problem. But such clarity is rare. Even after evaluators have completed a thorough research process and have computer printouts and interview transcripts stacked six inches high on every available space, they can still agonize over the question: What does it all mean?

It might seem unusual that this question could occur after all the research has been done. But, as earlier discussions indicated, the results from many of those steps may leave the researchers with indefinitive conclusions. When evaluators combine these less-than-conclusive results with the methodological limitations encountered during the project, the results often paint a fuzzy picture. The results are all in, but what does the picture show?

The task of answering questions about the fundamental effectiveness of any social program can make the other methodological problems encountered during the research process seem almost small by comparison. There are of course those rare cases when the collected information paints such a clear and unmistakable picture that the evaluator's judgment is merely a matter of stacking the data behind the inevitable conclusions. In situations like this, the need for individual judgment is minimal. But, as mentioned earlier, these are the rare "easy calls." The program went according to its plan; there are no significant problems to explain. The program is working smoothly, and evaluators have only to say just that.

More often, the results are not so obvious. There can be inconsistencies in the data patterns, and sometimes these variations go in different directions. The program might have had dramatic success with a few of its goals and significant failure with others. Some goals might be in the middle of this failure-success continuum, showing no apparent effectiveness and yet no obvious failure either. This kind of programmatic inconsistency is not unusual, and it is often frustratingly difficult for evaluators to summarize.

Total failure of a program is another, even harder story to tell. To be completely fair, evaluators have to look at the "failures" from a broad perspective because failure is a strong, absolute assessment. The notion of total failure means that *nothing* in the program succeeded. Nothing happened that should have happened. That comprehensive indictment means that despite all the efforts of the people involved and the expenditure of large sums of money, nothing of consequence happened. That kind of assessment is difficult to make. And, it is also *almost always wrong*!

As emphasized earlier, social programs are comprehensive undertakings. Something *always* happens with these activities. The results may be unplanned or even unwanted, but almost by definition, "something" is certain to happen. Evaluators should have this premise in mind during this final phase of their investigation.

A major task for evaluators, then, may be to explain the context of a program's *apparent* failure. It might be, for example, that the failure came more from inappropriate goals than poor programming. Evaluators should explain that if the administrators had established more appropriate goals, the program might have shown dramatic successes instead of failures.

A program's failure may also lie with the evaluation rather than the program content. The evaluators should look at the data carefully, with special attention on the evaluation's methodology. If the evaluators used weak measures, it would be unreasonable to make definitive statements about the program's failures. In this case, they should emphasize the measurement weaknesses and explain how those weak measures limit the credibility of the conclusions. If there were significant weaknesses in data-gathering or in the evaluation design, the researchers need to point these things out.

These alternative explanations for poor performance should not be regarded as excuses for a program's ineffectiveness. In most cases, the limitations imposed by factors such as time and money could weaken the evaluation to such an extent that evaluators have to conclude they do not "know" that the program is failing to perform. The qualifications in the evaluation should be realistic assessments, not lame excuses.

The underlying difficulty with this phase of the evaluation process is that it is so ambiguous. The other procedures generally have specific lists of things to do and not do. There are also procedures to handle problems that emerge. Unfortunately, there are no definitive lists for this final phase.

The evaluators have to review and reconsider everything they have done thus far. They also have to throw their professional experience into the final process, along with a large dose of common sense. What comes out of this should be a reasoned and productive assessment about the program's accomplishments and its overall effectiveness.

One way to help this difficult process along is to go through the judgment in segments rather than in one large jump. This gradual approach is especially helpful to inexperienced evaluators. After the work that went into the research, the last thing any evaluator wants is a report consisting of unsubstantiated assertions, vague generalizations, and a few personal observations. Researchers can avoid that kind of product if they are as careful in this final phase of the process as they were in the others.

An early (probably the first) segment in this judgment phase is the *goal analysis*. Evaluators should begin by categorizing each program goal as a success (the goal was achieved), a partial success (the goal was partly achieved), or a failure (the goal was not achieved). These initial assessments are possible as long as listed goals were specific. Evaluators should clarify which of these goals were established by the program and which, if any, were part of the evaluators' "implicit goal list."

Adequate supporting data should accompany the conclusions. It would be hard to overstate the need for sufficient data to support statements about the success or failure of the program's goals. Readers will consider every statement in the final section important, but their eyes and minds inevitably focus on whether the program goals were achieved. This is why final statements about goal performance need supporting data. When there are complaints about reports, they are usually challenges to the evaluators' interpretations of the program's goal performance. It is in the evaluators' best interests for initial interpretations to be firmly grounded in the data. Although goal analysis is only the beginning of the final interpretation, evaluators do not want readers to dismiss these statements with a casual "Well, that's just *their opinion.*" By now, the data should permit much more than opinions about what happened. The evaluators should have opinions, but these statements come later in the report. Readers should be convinced early that evaluators have enough information to support the statements they make.

It is usually a good idea to offer only basic data when assessing the program's goals. For example, state goal number one. Then state that the data show that the program succeeded or failed to meet its objective. Then move on to the next goal. Explanations about why these patterns of success and failure may have emerged come later.

The second component of the judgment phase can supply data on other, nongoal patterns found during the evaluation. These data form the "other major findings" in an evaluation report. Though these data do not usually deal with specific program goals, they are potentially important.

If the data-gathering process was open-ended — and often even if it was not — evaluations generate large quantities of information that have nothing directly to do with program goals. Those serendipitous patterns can turn out to be a vital component of the program and of the subsequent evaluation. On these points as well, the evaluators should have enough information to support whatever statements they make. Other findings can often turn a failing program into something of a triumph.

It is worth emphasizing that the evaluators' function is not to "find" some success in a program; but it is their function to do a complete job. In most evaluations, some information collected will inevitably deal with "positive" things that are happening as a result of the program's activities. Even a program that has not accomplished its goals might be providing a variety of positive experiences for people. Part of the evaluators' job is to describe the nature of those experiences.

It is important then that evaluators avoid giving any indication that they are trying to "protect" or in any way justify a "failing" program. The line between a premature assessment of failure and making an artificial case for a program's accomplishments can be a fine line.

After finishing the evaluation, researchers often have a variety of impressions, ideas, or "feelings" about the program. Sometimes these feelings involve people. Or they may have impressions about the overall efficiency of administrative procedures. Sometimes their ideas deal with inspirations about how to alter the program to make it function more effectively. Even if there is not enough information to support these personal assessments, they also belong in the final report. The evaluator can put these "unsubstantiated" statements into the third component of the evaluation.

Evaluators generally enter a program situation with training, experience, and a high degree of professional objectivity. During the research, if they develop "feelings" about some or all of the program's features, there are usually good reasons. The justification or explanation may not be in the data itself or even in the background information. But even if they are subjective and lack supporting data, those personal views and interpretations are potentially valuable. Evaluators would not be doing the people involved in the program any service by ignoring personal assessments.

This portion of the report can and should be a creative segment of the evaluation. Most administrators and funding agencies want to hear what evaluators thought, even when those statements are outside the framework of the formal analysis.

Finally, there is the culmination of the evaluation report, the all-important final conclusion. What evaluators write at this point summarizes everything that has gone before. They have to be extremely careful here and resist the understandable tendency to draw simple conclusions. Things are rarely simple in social programming.

Even if an organization met none of its intended goals, something happened. People started work, activities occurred, personal experiences took place, and inevitably lives were changed. The results may not have been intended or even wanted, but they did happen. These are "program effects," and they are what evaluators explain to the report's readers.

Success and failure are both complex terms. Evaluators have to remember this complexity when they write up the final assessment of a program. The evaluators' fundamental job has to be more than reaching a simple conclusion. Evaluators tried to *understand* the program. Now it is their job to convey that understanding to the report's readers.

The evaluators in the Meals on Wheels Program, for example, probably had a more difficult report writing task than they expected. They looked at the program's performance on its goal to "increase by 20 percent the psychological well-being of recipients" and they found an increase of 26 percent. Although the results initially looked good, the evaluators had to interpret these data in the context of an apparent selection bias. Only volunteers came into the meals program. This situation probably made a huge difference in what happened as a result of the program. Volunteers are more motivated than other home-bound elderly, and therefore they would be more likely to show higher psychological scores. It would not be reasonable to assume that these volunteer recipients of home meal services are similar to other older people in terms of the potential psychological improvement.

Furthermore, although the evaluators used a control group, it was not an especially appropriate one. Faced with time restrictions, the evaluators ended up using a comparative sample of older people in local senior centers. These more active people are very different from those getting meal deliveries. As a result, the strength of the comparisons between the two groups was not great.

On the positive side, the evaluators felt that their measurements and data-gathering were sound. They also had a number of anecdotes to support the data on the psychological well-being index; several people receiving meals volunteered to act as "telephone companions" for other, more physically infirm, individuals; a few meals recipients decided to take themselves off the list of recipients because, they said, "Other people need it more than I do"; and there were two cases where the recipients wanted to bake cookies and cakes for others.

The evaluators' final assessment of this goal can mention these stories and other relevant information that may not have been included in the initial presentation of data. As mentioned earlier, the notion of a "success" or a "failure" of individual program goals is rarely simple.

The "readability" of the report is another important element of evaluation. Evaluators should be thinking about this readability factor throughout the document, but it has special significance during the final narrative section. Few things can undo a competent evaluation quicker than poor writing. Grammatical and stylistic errors, sterile prose, and the use of scientific jargon can turn a good evaluation into a useless stack of paper. Unreadable reports have the same practical value as reports that were never done. Evaluators have to think about the relationship between good writing and a report's effectiveness. Evaluators should allow time to work on the quality of writing in that report. The prospect of spending time on the writing task is likely to have little appeal. Who wants to spend time that could be used for computer analysis looking for excessive use of the passive voice or editing out jargon. Evaluators may not want to spend this time, or they may not have it to spend.

There is also a possibility that evaluators may not know how to compose a readable report. A quick glance at social science journals will demonstrate that good writing is not common. If evaluators lack the tools to compose reports that are thorough yet concise, clear without being patronizing, and free from grammatical and stylistic errors, they should seek assistance. If evaluators cannot produce a readable document, they are wasting all those hours of data gathering and analysis.

Aesthetics are one additional part of the report's potential effectiveness. A professional appearance will not substitute for clarity in writing, but neat pages, attractive charts, and professional packaging provide an initial impression of a competent job. Competence is precisely the impression evaluators want to give.

A cautionary note is appropriate here. Even if the report looks good, the contents are readable, and the evaluation is a model of research competence, there are no guarantees that what the evaluators say will make any difference in what happens to a program. The grant may be awarded in spite of an evaluation that documented serious faults in a program, or the grant application may be turned down despite a glowing evaluation. Or the program managers may not give the document more than a cursory reading despite its competence and readability.

These outcomes do not mean that the evaluators failed. Evaluators whose sense of professional well-being rests upon definitive actions after they issue the final report are asking for disappointment. Evaluators' rewards have to come from a personal sense of accomplishment, a conviction that the project was done in the best possible fashion. Anything more is professional gravy.

It would be accurate to describe the final interpretive phase of the evaluation as something like sitting down to a good meal. This is where evaluators bring all the ingredients together. If everything was done properly, each written segment in this final phase of the evaluation will be like the courses in a good meal. Evaluators can savor every morsel because they know how much work went into it.

Selected Readings

Goldstein, M. S., Marcus, A. C., Rausch, N. P. (1978). "The Nonutilization of Evaluation Research." *Pacific Sociological Review,* 21 (January): 21–44.

This article is a good discussion of "usable" evaluation research. Though the author does not list writing skills, it was probably an oversight.

Safire, W. (1990). *Fumble Rules*. New York: Doubleday.
A quick review of basic grammatical rules and common errors. Few people who read this book will remain satisfied with their own writing.

CHAPTER SIX

Program Evaluation: A Case Study

A good means of summarizing, or "wrapping-up," the material from the preceding chapters is to review a real program evaluation. Working through the process with an actual case is also a good way to emphasize another point made several times in the preceding discussion: an evaluation is not a set of absolute rules applied in a rigid format.

The principles in a program evaluation have to be flexible, because evaluation projects rarely fit into precise molds. Experienced researchers know that each project has its own characteristics and is liable to produce its own problems. As a result, they have to handle each evaluation as though it were a journey to a new and uncharted area.

Although unique situations demand adjustments in the research process, it is seldom necessary to discard the whole plan. Evaluators simply have to decide how to adjust their initial framework to the situation. They may have planned, for example, to utilize interviews as the primary data collection technique. In spite of the considerable advantages from interviews, things could change dramatically when the researchers try to use this technique in the field. They may encounter unexpected situations that make it impossible to conduct interviews. The respondents may turn out to be far more suspicious of outsiders than anyone anticipated. Or the subject matter could be more sensitive than anyone thought. As a result, the interviews turn out to be more difficult to do than anyone anticipated. The research setting could be a location that makes it difficult to obtain enough trained interviewers. Any or all of these situations could delay the evaluation if the plan relies solely on interviews.

When new situations emerge, evaluators have to scrap their well-laid plans and consider the use of other procedures. Flexibility has to be evaluators' central guideline in working through the research process, from the planning stage through the final draft of the report.

Now to that actual case. The background of the situation is as follows. A nonprofit agency contacted an evaluator and asked for a formal program assessment. The program in question had operated for almost two years. The agency was applying for additional funding, and the granting agency, a private foundation, requested a formal evaluation before making a decision.

Except for basic office supplies and money for postage, there were no funds for the research. The agency gave the evaluator sixty days to complete the project, telling him to "do as much as you can" under the circumstances. And that is what he did.

This case study, with changes in names, describes an actual evaluation project completed several years ago. Because the agency involved had no funds for the evaluation, the evaluator agreed to volunteer his time. He also offered the services of his graduate students in that semester's Evaluation Research Seminar.

It turned out to be a wonderful opportunity for those students to get practical experience. They jumped into their individual research tasks with more enthusiasm than anyone had any right to expect.

Background

The evaluator's first step was to obtain the original grant proposal. The document indicated that the program, called the "Senior Legal Rights Program," began about eighteen months earlier. One intention of the program's designers was to compose and publish a legal manual for distribution to organizations and individuals. The manual would be a comprehensive document containing information on the legal problems facing older Americans. This manual would also serve as the basic resource for a cadre of trained older volunteers who would act as legal advocates for their peers. The training of those legal advocates was the other goal of this program.

The overall intent of the program, as expressed in the original grant proposal, was to "empower a group that has not had much power." The twin components of the legal manual and the trained volunteers were to be the catalyst for this community group's empowerment.

The private social service organization overseeing the program had a long history with "empowerment" programs. Their technique for developing community-based empowerment had been to get a particular program started and then turn it over to an appropriate local group. Once they turned over the control, this social service organization usually severed relationships with the program.

Because of this built-in separation process, the agency itself was not a large one. The local branch had an affiliation with a national organization but had only ten full-time employees. These ten individuals worked out of a crowded office, a single rented room in an older downtown office building.

The agency employees seemed to be overloaded with paper work; each individual frequently juggled grants for several programs at once. Except for the agency's director, the entire staff was on "soft money," meaning that they relied on the steady receipt of outside grants for operating funds. Everyone in the agency knew that if they did not obtain grants, there would be no jobs for most of them. They seemed to understand that situation and to accept it. Job insecurity was part of the working atmosphere. Surprisingly, their tenuous employment status did not seem to cause undue stress among the employees. It was simply "the way things were."

When the evaluator talked to the agency director, he was enthusiastic about the Senior Legal Rights Program. But the director did not appear any more committed to this particular program than to any of the others he was overseeing. As he explained during the initial interview, "We always have a lot of things going on around here, and it is impossible to keep up with all of them. I try to keep up, but you know how it is."

The director introduced the evaluator to the people who were directly responsible for the Senior Legal Rights Program (SLRP). The two women in charge of SLRP had been with the agency for a relatively short time. Maggie had been with the organization for three years, and Janet for only six months. This was the first project for which Janet had assumed direct responsibilities for program activities.

Maggie and Janet were both excited about the program. They showed the evaluator the legal manual written by volunteers. Lawyers who contributed their time checked the contents of the document for legal correctness. It was a large manual, some six hundred pages, carefully indexed and apparently written in a user-friendly fashion. The manual had sections on Medicare, Social Security payments, wills, and a variety of other legal issues concerning older citizens.

Maggie was going to handle the classroom training for the senior volunteers going through the training program. Janet attended to the various administrative details. She also acted as a backup trainer and handled the mail and phone requests for the manual.

Besides the formal training sessions, the agency mailed out copies of the manual to any interested parties who requested one. The cost for the manual was $15. Though there was no actual advertising program describing the manual or offering it for sale, they had mailed out "about three hundred" manuals by that point. Fortunately for the evaluator, the agency kept the names and addresses of everyone who sent for a copy.

After reviewing several other internal documents, the evaluator told Maggie and Janet that observers would attend as many formal training sessions as possible. Funding limitations forced the agency to cut back on the number of training locations. They had originally planned to have four training sites but ended up with two. One classroom training site was a federally funded high-rise apartment building in the central area of the city, and the other site was a community senior center in another neighborhood.

The evaluator decided to have several research assistants scan local newspapers and senior citizen newsletters for editorial and public comments on the program. Maggie and Janet also agreed to save correspondence and other material they received about the manual and about the training sessions.

At this early point in the evaluation, the SLRP appeared to be a carefully thought-out program. The organization was trying to serve a neglected community need (senior legal rights), and it was using an established social service model (group empowerment) to address that need. If it was successful with this program design, it would not be establishing yet another service agency. Older citizens would have the means to seek out and demand their own rights.

The program apparently had a sound foundation; the need was specific, there was a definite target audience for the service, and the organization had the experience and the staff to complete the project. All this seemed like a good start for a new program.

The Goals

The initial grant proposal was explicit about the goals of the Legal Rights Program. The agency director, along with Janet and Maggie, agreed that the three goals listed in that document accurately described what the agency wanted to accomplish. Though they agreed that the evaluation might uncover other program effects, they felt that the examination of the program's efforts should be directed at those three primary goals:

1. *Develop a legal rights manual for senior legal advocates.* This manual would contain information on most of the issues con-

fronted by older Americans. The writing in the manual would be free of the usual legal jargon and thus understandable and accessible to the layperson.

2. *Train initial groups of elderly volunteers who would act as legal advocates for their peers.* These individuals would receive adequate training in how to use the manual as a resource for that information. They would also have access to volunteer attorneys who would be willing to accept questions and/or referrals from those advocates.

3. *Develop a self-sustaining community support structure for the advocates.* After the initial training sessions, the agency would make provisions at every site for space, telephones, and office supplies. The agency would try to insure that these basic materials would be permanently available for the volunteer advocates.

At this early point in the process, the evaluator had no reason to list other goals for the program's assessment. The three listed goals seemed to be comprehensive. There was nothing in the literature or the evaluator's experience to indicate a need to look for other program effects. However, that need could emerge later in the analysis. To allow for that possibility, the data-gathering procedures would emphasize open-ended techniques. Other effects, if they existed, would show up in the data.

Measurement Devices

Finding appropriate measurements for the elements or variables contained in the program's goals turned out to be easier than expected. There were no unusual psychological traits or social attributes that might have caused problems in finding adequate measures. At this early point, the evaluator had to operationally define (i.e., translate into actual measurements) only three terms. He understood that it might be necessary to add to this list as the project progressed.

The three terms, and their operational definitions, were as follows:

a. *Legal advocates.* This concept included individuals who fulfilled two essential characteristics: they were willing to contribute at least fifteen hours a week as volunteer (unpaid) advocates; and they agreed to complete the ten-week advocate training.

b. *Support structure.* The "support structure" for the legal advocates is the material necessary for the volunteers to do their work.

Evidence that such a structure exists includes the actual existence of these materials or documentation of adequate monetary or other commitments from individuals and/or organizations. Those contributions and/or commitments can be either to the sponsoring organization or to the individual community sites. Evidence is needed to show that the necessary supplies and physical facilities will be available regularly.

c. *Legal rights manual.* The agency produced this legal manual to serve as a source of information on legal questions facing older people. The manual already exists, so this is not a question or measurement problem. But the agency intended that the manual be written in a style and format that would be accessible to the nonprofessional. Measuring the comprehensiveness and accessibility of the manual would require asking the potential advocates using it whether it contains the information they need and if they can interpret the contents without difficulty.

As mentioned, the evaluator did not have to devise measurements for any other terms at this point in the process.

Evaluation Design

The evaluator had to look at each goal when he selected the evaluation designs. It was as if each goal was a separate research project. It would not have been unusual if evaluating each goal required a different evaluation design.

As it turned out, none of the three goals required the use of an evaluation design. Since none of the goals predicted movement or change, there were no measured differences to explain. In other words, there was no change from point A to point B, and because there were no differences or changes, it was not necessary or even appropriate to use an evaluation design.

For example, one program goal for the SLRP concerned the intention to publish a legal rights manual. Assessing the success of that goal did not require the use of control groups, experimental groups, pretests or posttests. To find out if a legal rights manual was written, the evaluator had only to find evidence that the manual existed and that it was done in the intended style.

Assessing the success of this goal required only the evidence for a straightforward "yes" or "no." Even the stipulation that the manual be written clearly is another situation where a "yes" or "no" would suffice.

Here, as elsewhere, the absence of a formal design did not weaken the quality of the evaluation. If a formal evaluation design were necessary, then the strength of that design would play an important role in the methodological quality of the evaluation. If a design were inappropriate, it would not be used. The overall quality of the evaluation would rest on the other methodological procedures.

Data-Gathering

With the measurements set, the evaluator had to decide how the necessary data were going to be collected. After reviewing the measurements for the three goals and considering the possibility that other appropriate items might emerge during the research, the evaluator decided to use four research techniques. The use of four techniques would provide more comprehensive coverage of the program activities, and they would give the evaluator the ability to focus several techniques on the important measurements.

Program participants would fill out questionnaires either before or after their training. If there were enough time, the researchers would ask the participants to fill out the questionnaires both before and after the training, thus providing pre- and posttest data.

The information from the questionnaires would provide data on several important items. These data would be sources of comparison with data from other techniques. Since there was no apparent sensitivity with any of the questions, the questionnaire data should not have had any unusual validity or reliability problems.

Besides using the program participants, the evaluator planned to send a questionnaire to individuals who called or wrote to the agency for a copy of the legal rights manual. These survey responses from those who did not receive formal training in the manual's use would be an important addition to this component of the evaluation.

The researchers also hoped to conduct interviews with selected program participants, administrators, the trainer, and others who might have something to contribute to the program's evaluation. Most of the research time, though, would focus on the interviews with program participants. Researchers would be looking for information to supplement what they got from the questionnaires, especially on attitudes about the manual. The reaction to the manual was obviously a key element here. Reactions to the training sessions and the class content would be other areas of emphasis during these interviews.

During the formal training sessions, researchers would make unscheduled observations at the two training sites. They planned to sit in on the training sessions to gather information about content, trainer performance, and the participation by the individuals attending class. If possible, and if it did not cause internal problems, the researchers would also talk informally to individuals after the class sessions. These brief interviews would cover incidents that happened in class, the individuals' general reactions to the training, and other appropriate subjects.

Finally, the researchers would use official reports or media articles on the Senior Legal Rights Program. They would do as thorough a search as possible to look for discussions of the program.

The evaluator also planned to examine the scientific literature, looking for articles on related issues such as the legal problems of the elderly. Although he had not found anything that showed the existence of similar "elderly legal rights" programs anywhere in the country, he planned to continue looking for articles that might shed more light on the need for, or experience with, this type of program. He was also interested in the results that other organizations had had with this type of program design.

At this point, the research plan was complete. The researchers were ready to begin the information-collecting phase. Before going into the field, they decided that a "final check" of the design would be useful.

The Final Check

The final check is not a complete review of the whole evaluation plan. The procedure is more like filling out a shopping list, a relatively simple, painless process that insures the presence of essential items. This procedure permitted the evaluator to see at a glance if everything he needed for the evaluation was there. If it wasn't, there was still time for corrections.

The goals, the measurements of the various items, the data-gathering techniques, and the evaluation designs—all the evaluation methodology—should be on that list. If there are any significant gaps in the process, they would be obvious.

There is nothing mandatory about this final checklist, but it is a good idea, even for the experienced evaluator. Evaluators who use some type of final review have a variety of techniques for doing it, so the specifics are not important. The essential thing is that the evaluator give himself the chance to find and correct serious errors before the research process actually begins. Once the process starts, it may not be easy to make major additions.

In the checklist, shown in table 6.1, the evaluator assigned "scores" to each of the three methodological components: measurement, data-gathering, and design. Looking at the resulting totals gave the evaluator a quick, accurate look at the overall quality of the evaluation.

The scale used to assign scores for the three methodological components of the evaluation was as follows:

3 = excellent; no significant problems or weaknesses.
2 = generally good; some limitations exist, but these limitations are not considered serious.
1 = significant weaknesses or limitations.
0 = very weak, to the point of being almost unacceptable.

The checklist showed that the evaluation methodology seemed to be complete. The list of items included every goal that had to be examined. The evaluator had measures for all the necessary items. He also apparently would have enough data to assess each goal. None of the three goals needed an evaluation design.

There are no absolute or fixed standards for a "high quality" evaluation. A "6/6" or 100 percent score seems to indicate a perfect evaluation, but it has to be remembered that this is only an informal process. This or any other checklist can only be a guide at this early point, not an absolute assurance that the evaluation will be a good one.

At this point, though, it did not seem necessary for the evaluator to consider making any significant changes in the content or scope of the evaluation. He seemed to be equipped to go with what he had. And that was what he did.

Table 6.1 • *An Evaluation Check Sheet*

Goals	Measures	Data-gathering	Evaluation design	Score
1. Develop manual	Manual	Documents	none	6/6
2. Train advocates	Number of advocates	Questions	none	6/6
3. Support structure	Existence of sites	Interviews	none	6/6

The data-gathering process went very well. The program's participants had no apparent problems with the presence of researchers in the training sessions and neither did Janet or Maggie. The two program managers provided everything the researchers needed in the way of information. Overall, it was a thoroughly enjoyable experience for everyone, both professionally and personally.

Despite the lack of funds and time, this Legal Rights Program received a thorough and professional evaluation. About five months after the researchers finished the data-gathering, the evaluator wrote the formal assessment for the funding agency. This step was more difficult than he anticipated.

The private foundation wanted a report they could use for their decision about the funding for this project. Readability was especially important. The foundation wanted "something we could read and understand for a change." That is what the evaluator tried to provide.

Writing that evaluation report was the final step in the evaluation. The actual report submitted to the foundation, with some editing to preserve anonymity, follows. Remember the limitations the evaluator faced on this project: no money and very little time. Look at the evaluation report from this perspective and decide whether its components represent sound evaluation principles.

As with any evaluation, the intention of the evaluator was to provide as thorough and objective an assessment as possible under the existing circumstances. Readers can judge whether or not he succeeded.

The Senior Citizen as Legal Advocate: A Program of Empowerment

The general variety of problems that many of the nation's older citizens face on a daily basis has been frequently publicized over the past few years. Although it would not be accurate to argue that the public completely understands either the frequency or the severity of these difficulties, it does seem reasonable to talk about an increasing general concern about the elderly's situation in American society. Indeed, interest in some aspects of the aging process, notably the topics of death and retirement, has approached a fervor not seen in the United States since hula hoops went around.

The response of the various public agencies, private groups, and politicians at all levels, was predictable: more programs, more pronouncements, more platitudes and, when it was available, more money. Efforts to deal with the problems of the elderly have, to put it mildly, increased fairly quickly. All types of programs and procedures are emerging as more individuals and groups seek to climb aboard the "greying" train. What about the net result of this activity?

That question is difficult to answer, at least with any degree of certainty. Some problems afflicting many older people, such as physical ailments, trying to maintain an acceptable standard of living, and finding enjoyable outlets for leisure time, are obviously still there. About the only definitive statement possible about the extent of any improvements with these problem areas is that older citizens can now benefit from, or confront (depending on your perspective), a variety of potential outlets for resolving these situations.

Although some of these potential outlets may prove to be less than beneficial, the problem for many older citizens these days is not whether it is possible to have something done, but how to discover the correct procedure and the correct agency for getting it done.

Several years ago, a private organization with a history of involvement in social welfare activities designed a program to deal with the legal issues surrounding older people. Writing wills, getting the appropriate Social Security benefits, and applying for Medicare are some of the many legal questions confronting older Americans. This program wanted to train older laypeople in the details of various laws and programs, ultimately equipping these people to serve as legal advocates for their peers.

The program had no intention of producing professional paralegals. It merely wanted individuals who, with access to appropriate resource material, could help older people locate appropriate sources for solutions to their problems. Legal assistance is one service that many older people cannot afford. The intent of the Senior Legal Rights Program (SLRP) was, in effect, to empower the elderly and to provide them with the tools to act for themselves in dealing with their legal concerns.

This "Senior Legal Rights Program" had several specific goals in its initial design:

1. *The construction and distribution of a legal rights manual.* They wanted this document to be available and to have information on programs and laws of particular concern to older citizens (e.g. Medicare, Social Security, ERISA, etc.). They also wanted it written in a way that would be easy for the layperson to understand. They wrote the manual to be a problem-solving resource for questions confronting older citizens. Distribution of the document was

to be made to all interested citizens and groups, and also to those who attended the formal training sessions. The charge for the manual was fifteen dollars.

2. *The establishing of sites for the training of volunteers.* The program designers initially planned four sites, but this goal had to be scaled back because of insufficient funding. The final schedule called for training classes at two sites, a subsidized high-rise apartment for the elderly near the city's downtown area and a multi-purpose elderly center in another neighborhood of the same city. The programmers did no initial screening of participants; the publicity before the beginning of formal classes simply urged "all interested parties" to attend.

As a result, the characteristics of the participants were not representative of the city's elderly population.

- Just over 80 percent of the participants were female. This result is different from that in many other studies that document the higher participation of males in such activities.
- Thirty-three percent of the group were married; 46 percent were widows or widowers, and 21 percent were single.
- Only 12 percent of the participants had any college education. Twenty-five percent of them had less than a grammar school diploma. This concentration of participants from the lower educational strata turned out to be important in understanding patterns that emerged during the later analyses.
- Most of the people attending the sessions were between the ages of sixty-four and seventy-two; the oldest was eighty-three. Most of the participants described their health as at least "fairly good."

3. *The promotion of an active group of legal advocates.* The training sites were selected with the idea that they would serve as permanent training centers, thus providing the advocates with the necessary office space, telephone equipment, and resource material. The sponsoring agency initially planned to stay at each site until the advocate groups were working and seemed firmly established.

This Senior Legal Rights Program was unique; it was not yet another organizational alternative to the problems of older Americans. Instead, it was a device to provide a means for older citizens to solve their own problems. SLRP intended to give the sixty-five and older age group a means of self-determination that the larger society, whether intentional or not, has largely co-opted over recent years.

The Evaluation

"Evaluation Research" is a term for a process that applies social science research techniques to the study of a social program and its activities. The purpose of evalution research is to find out how well a program is functioning and to explain why. As anyone who has been involved with this process could attest, the primary obstacle is devising an acceptable definition for "functioning."

To answer the questions here with some accuracy required us to generate information from as many sources as possible. Although we used a variety of data-gathering procedures, some of them were more effective than others:

1. *Participant observation.* This technique puts the researcher into the actual social situation. Our observers, graduate students in sociology and trained in the use of field methods, were sent to the two training sites. They sat in on most of the sessions. To reduce the potential for any discomfort their presence may have caused, we told the program participants that the observers were there to "learn how the classes operate." The observers took detailed field notes at all these sessions, and these data were an important part of the written assessment.

2. *Interviews.* Researchers held semi-structured interviews with a selected sample of the trainees. We chose to do these interviews, twenty-four in all, to obtain information not available from the classroom observations. The information sought in these interviews included the attitudes of the trainees about the class, their reasons for attending the sessions, and how they felt about the trainers. This information was essential to adequately assess the trainee attitudes and reactions.

3. *Telephone interviews.* The researchers had neither the time nor the funds to interview all of the program participants. On several occasions, we telephoned participants and asked them a few questions similar to those asked in the face-to-face interviews. Although these telephone sessions usually lasted no more than five minutes, they produced a surprising amount of irritation and suspicion. After this consistently negative attitude pattern emerged, we stopped the use of the technique.

4. *Documents.* Document analysis proved to be the least effective of all the data-gathering techniques used during the evaluation. We set up a review procedure and watched all the local newspapers and even the institutional newsletters for some mention of the program in advocacy training. Except for a few informational items, the sources reviewed did not mention the legal rights program or the issues involved.

5. *Mailed questionnaires.* To examine the reactions of the people who obtained the legal rights manual through the mail,

we mailed a three-page questionnaire to everyone who sent for the document. Four hundred twelve questionnaires eventually went out and 124 came back. Although we have no reason to suspect any bias in that sample, a response rate of 31 percent does require us to be cautious in any generalizations from these data.

The major problems confronting the evaluation were typical ones: insufficient funds and not enough time. We did not have the money for complete coverage of the training sessions, not enough time for more than a few interviews, and not enough time or money for a second mailing of the questionnaires.

Even with these limitations, we have high confidence in the reliability of the data. The data have a consistency that argues against any criticism about inadequate size. It seems reasonable to argue that even the low number of cases in some categories adequately represents the characteristics of the total population.

Results

One primary goal of the SLRP was the development of legal advocates, individuals trained to be resources of information to assure that older citizens received whatever benefits and rights they had coming. Was this goal met?

From the information generated at the two training sites, the answer is a definite "no."

Despite the willingness of several individuals to volunteer their personal time, there was no evidence at the conclusion of the observation period that *any* potential advocates had emerged. There were some isolated examples of individuals who claimed they helped friends or relatives with problems, but no clear or sustained pattern of such assistance surfaced. As we later found out from interviews, few of the trainees ever had intentions of becoming volunteer legal advocates.

The pattern in table 6.2 supports the early impression by our field observers that the trainees' commitment to the advocacy idea was extremely low. These early impressions came from observed patterns, such as sporadic attendance at the sessions, the lack of any real interest in learning how to use the manual, and the obvious individual concern with getting answers to personal questions.

We looked for other means to test this initial conclusion and settled on the notion of whether the trainees bought their own copy of the manual. These people used the manuals made available in class, but if they wanted one to take home, they had to buy it.

We reasoned that the purchase of the manual showed evidence of a more-than-passing interest in advocacy training. As table 6.3 shows, the answers given to this question supported the conclusion that interest in advocacy among the participants was low.

Although it is possible that the fifteen-dollar cost of the manual was a factor in this decision not to buy the book, we had no indication that money played the decisive role. A common reply given by the various participants when we specifically asked about the manual was similar to, "It was something the trainer used."

With all this information, limited though the sample size may be, it seems reasonable to conclude that the participants in these training sessions had little interest in becoming advocates. Our field observations support the further conclusion that the participants had no idea that volunteer advocacy was the *raison d'etre* of the training session.

Table 6.2 • *Willingness to Become Legal Advocates*

"Would you be willing to contribute from six to ten hours each week to serve as a legal advocate?"

	Yes	No	Maybe*
Site 1 (high-rise) (N = 8)	33%	12%	55%
Site 2 (community center) (N = 14)	21%	50%	29%

*The conditions set by the respondents for their participation usually involved the presence of their continued good health or the absence of any conflicting responsibilities.

Table 6.3 • *Another Indication of Willingness to Become an Advocate*

"Do you own your own copy of the legal rights manual?"

	Yes	No
Site 1 (high-rise) (N = 8)	0%	100%
Site 2 (community center) (N = 14)	7%	93%

At various times in both locations, we asked a series of people why (they thought) the training session existed. Some illustrative replies:

"To try to get more for yourself."
"I guess to answer our questions."
"They are good for dispensing information."
"This is not a program but a thought-provoking center."
"There is no purpose."

This pattern of responses indicated that these attitudes probably had not come from the experiences these people had in the training sessions; they brought these negative perceptions about the class with them. It would have taken a major effort by the trainer to turn these people, who, in effect, wandered into those classes, into practicing advocates.

This absence of commitment is the key to understanding the program's lack of success in producing advocates. But this trainee disinterest reflects on the absence of an effective screening procedure more than on the trainee motivation levels.

Yet there is also reason for some criticism of the training itself. The agency designed those sessions, two hours a day, twice a week, for about ten weeks, to train individuals in the use of the legal manual. Leaving aside for the moment the notion of the motivation of the participants, it is fair to ask whether they eventually learned how to use that manual.

When less than a third of the trainees felt ready to work with the manual at the close of the formal training cycle, we have to consider the possibility that the classroom sessions were not productive. After some discussion and a review of the data from the classroom observations, that was our conclusion. None of the sessions at either of the training sites showed any consistent

Table 6.4 • *Use of the Legal Rights Manual*

"Are you familiar enough with the legal rights manual to use it to find answers to questions you might get from other people?"

	Yes	No
Site 1 (high-rise) (N = 8)	25%	75%
Site 2 (community center) (N = 14)	29%	71%

emphasis on what "advocacy" was about and how the manual fit into the program's central goal.

At one site, the trainer did not even mention the term "advocacy" for several weeks. When the topic did come up, the trainer gave a series of often conflicting definitions. There was no formal structure that gave participants the information to understand precisely why they were attending those classes. It was no surprise that participants had their own reasons for attending.

The classes themselves were largely unstructured and lacking in specific legal orientation. It was apparent to the observers that the instructor had no strong skills in teaching techniques. The sessions, designed to train advocates, rapidly turned into information retrieval experiences. People came to the sessions with personal questions or problems. After they got their answers, they usually left, never to return.

In fairness to both the trainees and the trainer, the composition of the classes was undoubtedly the underlying cause for the absence of trainee interest. Since the design of the program provided no structure for screening out unsuitable or unmotivated individuals, the classes consisted largely of people with no strong interest in legal advocacy.

Finally, what about the legal rights manual? Assessing the reaction to this document depends on the audience. There is no doubt that the people who purchased the manual through the mail or by phone thought it was a valuable resource. Seventy-five percent of those responding to our questionnaire showed that they would purchase the manual again; less than 6 percent considered the money they spent as "wasted."

The reservation we have about concluding that this component of the program was completely successful is that 72 percent of the buyers were *under* the age of sixty-five. Responses to the mailed questionnaires showed that these manual purchasers were primarily using the document as a resource in their work with the elderly. The manual then is apparently serving the needs of older citizens, but in an indirect rather than direct fashion. Although this is not an undesirable situation, it does not go along with the initial intentions of the Senior Legal Rights Program.

There is no need to review the program's failure to establish any permanent, self-sustaining sites. The lack of success in training advocates meant that no permanent sites were needed. Unfortunately, it was not possible for us to look at questions that would have been of considerable interest, those concerning the long-term commitment of volunteer legal advocates and the extent of community support for the notion of senior legal advocacy.

Conclusions

Considering all the information available, it is our feeling that the Senior Legal Rights Program, at least as it was implemented in this particular situation, has been unsuccessful. Although a variety of factors made the program's goals almost unattainable from the beginning, the fact remains that after eight months of effort, no volunteer advocates emerged and no permanent training sites were established.

It is reasonable to argue that this failure should be considered as a fundamental weakness in how the planners applied the elements of the idea rather than with the notion of "self-help, legal advocacy" itself. The program people allowed, indeed they encouraged, every interested individual to attend those training sessions. The planners did not establish any qualifications for potential trainees, and they did not request any personal commitments from those attending.

The subsequent training sessions consisted primarily of people whose interests were not in advocacy. There was also a question of potential competence for advocates as well; as we discovered later, almost a quarter of the trainees at the two sites could neither read nor write.

With these structural weaknesses, it is fair to argue that this noble experiment did not adequately test the feasibility of training a cadre of elderly legal advocates to service the needs of the over-sixty-five population. With proper training for the instructors, a thorough screening of potential participants, and the availability of adequate work sites, the idea might be successful.

It might also be useful to consider paying salaries to the advocates instead of relying on volunteer availability. Even minimum wage salaries would generate more, and probably better qualified, applicants. The number of qualified applications would also increase if some form of community recognition for "graduates" existed. Either way, the notion that there is a pool of qualified senior citizens readily available for any and all community tasks has been successfully challenged again.

In sum, this attempt at a Senior Legal Rights Program did not work as anyone intended or hoped. It is conceivable that with several corrective measures, the program and the underlying concept could be successful.

Epilogue

The possibility that an evaluator could "go native" turned out to be very real here. The evaluator developed a strong friendship with both

Maggie and Janet during what turned out to be almost a year-long research program. That friendship made it difficult to submit what turned out to be a generally unfavorable report. Because of that report, although the decision probably stemmed from other factors as well, the sponsoring foundation did not renew funding for the Senior Legal Rights Program. Both Janet and Maggie lost their jobs with the agency as a result, and both went into other careers. They were exceptionally dedicated and competent individuals.

The last time anyone looked, no organization had picked up on the possibilities of elderly advocacy. It may be another idea whose time has not yet arrived.

Selected Readings

Wholey, J. S. (1987) Using program theory in evaluation: New directions for program evaluation. San Francisco, CA: Jossey-Bass.
This book provides a good understanding of the interplay between theory and evaluation.

Although a number of professional journals regularly publish articles dealing with program evaluation, readers looking for regular publication as well as discussion of the issues related to evaluation research might find the following journals especially helpful:

Journal of Evaluation Research
Evaluation and Program Planning
Evaluation Review
Journal of Social Service Research

CHAPTER SEVEN

And in Conclusion

The previous chapters have provided the outline for comprehensive and effective program evaluations. The discussions covered many topics and issues, but there are sometimes a few loose ends, which is why books need a concluding chapter.

One loose end is financial accountability. Even social programs have to account for their money. The days when "money is no object" are long gone, probably forever.

Using an accounting perspective on a social program raises some interesting and difficult questions. Although financial discussions are often handled by "numbers experts," it is in everyone's best interest if program evaluators understand the issues involved when financial topics are discussed. Those discussions influence whatever conclusions are made about the program.

Cost-Benefit Analysis

Since this is an era of declining resource bases coupled with increasing financial exigencies, it was virtually inevitable that there would be a demand that the nonprofit sector devise a means for assessing their financial as well as their organizational performances. Americans have become very dollar conscious in the past few years, especially when discussions involve organizations that receive tax dollars. Nonprofit social programs may not be "making money," but the public is beginning to insist these activities demonstrate that what they are doing is "worth the money."

Clearly, a process for measuring a program's financial efficiency is desirable. Even without the current concern over public expenditures, it is reasonable to question the desirability of suporting programs that waste money. The problem, then, is how to determine if money is being wasted.

Number manipulation is confusing to many people, but there is an appealing clarity to the results of that manipulating. People might not understand what the numbers mean and what exactly was done with them, but when the figures are posted, those they understand — or think they do. Who is the best candidate for a job? It is possible to sort out the interviews and call the references, but easier to just hire the individual with the best scores on the employment exam.

We believe that numbers can tell us everything. They give us what we want, with the clarity and convenience we love. Numbers may not tell the *complete* story, or they may convey *unrealistic* pictures. But who argues with numbers?

The numbers fixation fits into the evaluation process beautifully. We believe that a social program with a score of 98 *has* to be better than a program with a score of 36. A program that is showing $2.00 in benefits for every $1.00 of expenditures *has* to be helping someone. Even if there is no dollar profit and no money in the cash register, those positive numbers are reassuring.

It is conceivable that the numbers are telling accurate stories and that the interpretations people draw from those numbers are correct. But those are only possibilities; they are not certainties. Numbers can be useful but only when the people who are using them understand where those figures came from, what they represent, and what the inherent limitations are. Without that understanding, the use of numbers can lead to serious errors in judgment. It would be helpful to start at the beginning of this topic rather than at the end.

Cost-benefit analysis is another criterion for assessing social programs. The process is not used as a substitute for other evaluation data; it is, or it should be, a complementary type of analysis. In a cost-benefit analysis, dollars are the focal point. The success or failure that a program has in meeting its goals plays no role in this analysis. A successful program could give a poor showing in a cost-benefit analysis; it is also possible that a program that failed to meet any of its goals would look good in a cost-benefit analysis.

Cost-benefit review is usually part of a comprehensive evaluation rather than a separate process. When an agency asks the question, "How well is this program doing?" it often expects some type of financial analysis to be part of a comprehensive answer. Cost-benefit analysis looks at the relative efficiency of program activities by assigning dollar figures to both "costs" and "benefits," but the dollar amounts applied to social program activities seldom mean much standing by themselves.

How much does it cost to deliver the benefits of the Senior Legal Rights Program? Even if the evaluator could document a $300 cost figure per advocate, that amount would be meaningless. Is $300 a high or low amount for that kind of training? Obviously, it is impossible to say without more information. Dollar amounts are meaningful only when compared to something else, something that provides a basis of comparison.

The figures on the Senior Legal Rights Program could be contrasted with an educational training program. If we know it costs $300 to train a legal advocate and $2,000 to train a computer operator, we can arrive at some decision about how efficient the Legal Rights Program was.

We can also contrast the efficiency of the Legal Rights Program this year as compared with last year. As long as comparative figures are available, it is possible and reasonable to arrive at decisions about relative efficiency. These comparisons provide grant agencies and policymakers enough information to assess this component of a social program's performance.

Several indices are commonly used in cost-benefit analysis. They are not complicated, and most use the same basic ingredients in their calculations. One frequently used figure is the "cost minus benefits" index. The index name explains its basic computation. The total costs of a program are subtracted from its documented benefits.

If the Senior Legal Rights Program had a 1994 budget of $75,000, and the program generated $45,000 in benefits that year, the program would show a "net loss" of $30,000. Its index for that year would be −$30,000. This may or may not be a "good" figure. On the other hand, if the benefits totaled $100,000 for the year, the cost minus benefits index for that year would be +$25,000. Once again, this may or may not be a "good" figure.

The value of this or any other index lies in the comparisons discussed earlier. Comparing the figures from the Senior Legal Rights Program with those of another program or comparing program figures from different years could provide a means of assessing those amounts. If the Legal Rights Program steadily improved its performance on an index over several years, this would show up well in the analysis.

If a foundation were trying to decide which applicant organizations deserved funding, it might face a situation where every program applying for money had a positive program evaluation. In cases like this, the foundation could use the results of a cost-benefit index to see how efficiently the programs were doing their work. Presumably a program with a cost-benefit index of +$25,000 is doing a "better" job than a program with an index of −$50,000.

There are problems with these figures and with the figures from *any* cost-benefit index. But there is another common index to discuss before examining these fundamental problems. The cost/benefit ratio is another popular index. Here the total dollar cost is divided by the total dollar benefit. The index can also be computed another way, by dividing benefits by costs. Either way, the results presumably provide a measure of the program's relative efficiency.

If the costs of the Legal Rights Program total $75,000 and the benefits are precisely the same amount, the index would have a value of 1 (i.e., $75,000 ÷ $75,000 = 1). Another way of interpreting that result is that the program delivers $1.00 of benefits for every $1.00 of costs.

On the other hand, if the value of benefits comes to only $37,500, the index should have a value of 2 (i.e., $75,000 ÷ $37,500 = 2). This 2 means that it costs $2.00 to deliver $1.00 in benefits — not a very attractive index to bring before a funding agency!

The appeal of this particular index is apparent. It provides a built-in comparison, giving interested parties an idea of how "internally efficient" a program is. There is an immediate basis for judgment about a program's efficiency.

Both ratios put social programs on a competitive economic scale similar to those used for business enterprises. If a social program has a high efficiency, returning $2.00 for every $1.00 in expenses, for example, or shows a higher net benefit than some other program, it is seen as doing something right. If the figures show a low rate of return, the program is likely to be regarded as doing something wrong. And if something is wrong, like any other "business," the managers have to consider making corrections. The program should reduce its expenses or increase its benefits. Or maybe it should go out of business.

Researchers use other cost-benefit indices besides the two mentioned here. Although these other measures have some unique advantages and different interpretations, it is more useful at this point to explain the components common to the various indices. An understanding of these procedures gives evaluators the ability to understand what these indices can do *for* and *to* a program's evaluation.

The concept of "cost" is a central component in a cost-benefit index and is easy to misunderstand. At first glance, computing the cost of a program does not sound like an impossible or even an especially complex task. Adding salaries, building rental, utilities, equipment, supplies, and other miscellaneous items is routine. So, calculating the total costs for a program does not seem difficult.

With a small program, the process probably is easy, at least by comparison. In a ten-person social agency, for example, most of a program's costs should be obvious. There are salaries for the people who show up in the office every day, and it is easy to document where the money for office equipment and supplies goes, because all the material is on the shelves in the back room. Supplies and employees are all in one place. There are usually no hidden costs in small organizations. It is not likely that such an organization could devise a rationale for a $450 toilet seat, however comfortable it might be.

The notion of program costs can raise a host of difficult questions and issues when large organizations, encompassing a variety of activities, are involved. In these cases, the cost picture is rarely as clear. Many financial accounts exist, and money flies around with a speed and complexity that makes it difficult for even accountants to understand let alone follow.

The notion of "indirect costs" is part of an accounting process that springs up in many cost-benefit analyses involving larger programs. Indirect costs are charges for services shared by every activity in the organization. The idea is simple. The organization provides support services for the "line," or field, activities. The administrative and other functions of the agency are permanent, or "fixed," features, a set of services for the on-going and frequently transient social programs that take place out in the field.

A large social service agency often has many different programs operating simultaneously. Each individual program may have only a few employees working strictly on that program, while paper work is done by the main office personnel. The organization's administrative offices provide necessary logistical support for program activities, such as personnel services, issuing paychecks, and handling governmental relations.

The agency also has to pay for building depreciation, utilities, and postage, and the programs pay for these things directly or in some cases indirectly. When the Senior Legal Rights Program applied for funds, one item on the proposed budget was "indirect costs." Those costs are the (reasonable) contribution the program, in this case the Legal Rights Program, makes to the larger organizational structure. Each program legitimately pays its share of the larger organization's costs, because each program gets a share of its services.

Depending on the size of the organization and the budget of the individual program, the amount of these indirect costs could be considerable. When the budgetary process is finished, a program that has an initial budget of $75,000 in direct costs could show a final budget of $145,000. Indirect costs in the range of 40 to 70 percent of direct costs are not unusual or unreasonable.

Although it is tempting to picture sinister forces hiding behind indirect costs, their calculation and use are a legitimate accounting practice. If the costs of the Legal Rights Program did not include indirect costs, the program would receive the benefit of the sponsoring agency's services without paying for them. Someone has to pay those costs.

When people raise objections to indirect costs, they are usually questioning the inherent subjectivity of the calculating process. That flexibility or subjectivity allows considerable potential for abuse. What amount of cost should be absorbed by a particular program? How much is within reason? Questions about these figures can, and often do, generate considerable discussion and disagreement.

Sometimes there is no reason for disagreement. On formal grant applications, the funding agency may specify an acceptable amount for indirect costs. As mentioned earlier, levels of from 50 to 75 percent of program costs are common. In these cases, there might be no reason to be concerned about the accountant's discretionary power over the calculation of indirect costs.

There would be reason to be concerned, though, if no specific stipulation about the size of indirect costs exists, or if the resulting figures are to be part of a later comparative cost analysis. In either situation, evaluators have to be alert to the possibility that costs are being "dumped" on a program for reasons that have nothing to do with sensible accounting procedures.

If the administrator of the national organization that houses the Senior Legal Rights Program has some reason to support the program, he would want the program's numbers to look good. He might arrange the books so that the SLRP would assume only a small proportion of the organization's building expenses. Or he might eliminate all indirect costs for the program entirely. Either way, the SLRP would show up very well in a cost-benefit analysis.

On the other hand, if that administrator does not like the SLRP, he might load its budget with a series of indirect costs that would insure an unfavorable cost-benefit analysis, such as additional staff salaries and benefits, accelerated building depreciation, and increased support services. The list of potential items can lengthen quickly. It can be difficult to dispute the amounts shown for these items, especially for someone who is not an accountant.

Indirect costs are not the only potentially questionable item in a program's budget. One accounting practice common in some levels of government is "ghost payrolling," This interesting procedure does not imply that spirits from another world are working at the desks.

Ghost payrollers are those whose salaries are paid from areas other than where they are (presumably) working.

Several individuals might be assigned to program A's payroll even though they have nothing to do with that particular program. They might work in another office or on another program, or they may have the good fortune to be the brother-in-law of the organization's president. Sometimes there is criminal intent with practices such as ghost payrolling, but not always. Things like this often occur because it is the only way to work around rigid financial procedures.

Perhaps the agency needs to add another employee, but at this point in the fiscal year, there is no money in the appropriate account. There is money in the organization, but not in the account that covers what this new employee is going to do. So the money is found somewhere else. Someone may find enough spare funds in the account of program A, so the name of the new staff member goes into that program's budget, and the salary is now part of its program costs. The new employee is now a "ghost payroller."

Although the people in program A will probably never set eyes on this new employee, he will be working somewhere and doing something. This procedure might be questionable from a strict accounting or ethical perspective, but it has advantages. For one thing, having this flexibility permits a more efficient hiring process. In the long run, what difference does it make on which program payroll a name appears, as long as the people involved are doing their jobs?

Evaluators have to take a more narrow view, however, because someone has to look at the situation from the perspective of the individual program. Ghost-payrolling, or any other "creative" accounting practice, can turn an efficient program into what appears to be a money-devouring operation. Program A, for example, could turn into what looks like a nest of free-loaders, all because they had some excess funds. The evaluator is often the one who has the task of looking closely at program costs. Even when creative accounting practices exist, it should be possible to resolve the situation, assuming of course, that no one is trying to hide anything.

As hard as it may be to arrive at a reasonable cost figure, this is the easier part of the equation. Assigning a dollar value to a program's benefits can challenge anyone's power of creativity. Invariably, the significant weakness in any cost-benefit analysis involves calculating program benefits.

There are situations when the dollar amounts for benefits seem fairly clear. For example, suppose that the Metropolis Economic Center provides job training for welfare recipients. The program's primary goal is to "get people off welfare rolls and onto payrolls." The federal government underwrites the $5,000 per person cost of training people for jobs in the service sector. After the six-month training cycle, managers say that graduates will find jobs paying at least $20,000 a year.

The direct costs of the program include the training and some additional personal expenses of the trainees. These expenditures along with the indirect costs mean that it costs a total of $6,000 per person for job training. As for benefits, the state government saves the $10,000 a year welfare benefits for each individual who gets a job. In addition to this, these graduates will pay taxes on their yearly earnings. In this particular case, the dollar value of the program's benefits equals the welfare savings plus the new taxes paid. The cost-benefit index results should be positive.

Unfortunately, the value of benefits is not so obvious in most social programs. Social program activities often concentrate on individual and group activities that do not readily lend themselves to precise benefit calculations. The Senior Legal Rights Program is a good example.

The major thrust of that program was "empowerment of the elderly." Empowerment is one important benefit of the program activities, but what is the dollar benefit of empowerment? That commodity may not be worth anything to anyone other than the elderly people directly involved. Even these individuals would be hard pressed to assign a monetary value to "feeling more in control of your life."

If the advocacy training classes produced a high level of excitement within the elderly community and resulted in a greater sense of "individual self-worth," the question to answer would be, "How much is self-worth going for on the open market these days?" It would be hard for anyone to stand in front of a funding agency and argue that an increase in personal self-worth was worth $10, or $10,000 or even that it was "valuable." So where do these figures come from?

Someone recently challenged an economist to come up with a dollar figure for a happy marriage. He did. He cited a court case to support the figure he used. In that case, the jury assigned a dollar value to a marriage that had broken up. "We can come up with a dollar figure for anything," the economist insisted. "A pint of blood, personal happiness, you name it, and we can put a price on anything. On life itself!"

That economist's confidence is not unusual. Putting prices on social attributes may be open to debate, but that debate is usually about the size of the figure not the process itself. There is substantial agreement for the idea that there is a dollar value for everything. "Everything has its price" is part of the contemporary American mindset.

The federal regulation permitting organizations to sell the "right to pollute" is a good example. Businesses that have cleaned up their production process can now sell their right to pollute the air to businesses that have not improved their own production process. What is clean air worth? The United States now has a cost figure for that seemingly impossible question.

Evaluators can argue with assigning dollar values to social activities, but they will probably lose. People in general and funding agencies in particular like the idea of numerical figures. So instead of fighting a losing battle, evaluators should direct their attention to the "reasonable-ness" of the figures used. That chore is difficult enough, but there are other concerns as well. For one, the idea of "indirect costs" has a corresponding benefit category. Calling it "indirect benefits" is as appropriate as any other designation. Virtually any social program has outcomes (benefits) that cannot be traced directly to the program. The Senior Legal Rights Program, for example, may indirectly influence the attitudes about aging held by individuals within various families. Because family members now see their older relatives excited about living, these family members may begin to view aging in a more positive way.

Though it would be difficult to trace these changing attitudes directly to the Legal Rights Program, the potential for this relationship is there. The evaluator should try to assess this potential relationship when discussing the "value" of this program's benefits. So when dollar benefits are assigned, these indirect benefits could add to the program's "value."

The job training program for welfare recipients could indirectly affect the school grades of the children in those families. When people go to the training sessions and then ultimately get good jobs, their children have a chance to see the benefits that schooling can bring. They translate this experience into a need to do better at school. Then, because they ultimately receive a better education, these children need less supportive social services throughout the rest of their lives. Putting all these things together, the amounts add up quickly, and the total dollar benefits could be considerable.

The nature of these benefits is indirect though, and unless the research design is powerful, the rationale for the connection may not be strong. But if the survival of a program depends on its cost-benefit "efficiency," these "indirect" benefits may determine that survival.

Another difficult issue in calculating the benefit portion of cost-benefit indices involves the question of short-term versus long-term benefits. Determining what effects a program has requires establishing a definite time frame for examining those effects. When doing an evaluation, there is a tendency to focus on the program's immediate benefits. What did the program do *this year?* What were the improvements during the past year?

Evaluators look for evidence about what a program did recently. They do not often consider the possibility that some benefits may not show up for some time, even for several years. People's horizons seldom extend much past the next year. It is not easy to argue to a funding agency that a preschool program might take years to produce measurable results, but occasionally it's necessary to make that argument.

In the earlier example of the meals program, the possibility was raised that home-delivered meals could reduce the need for institutionalization. Even if this prediction proved accurate, the reduction in institutionalization rates would not show up for years. Although the evaluator could not provide evidence of this relationship in the limited research time frame, the potential benefits of this effect should be a part of the discussion. The calculation of "long term" benefits could turn out to be one of the most important things evaluators do when they compute the cost-benefit analysis.

Another issue in cost-benefit computations involves the "level" at which the cost-benefit analysis occurs. When evaluators look at a program's accomplishments and its associated costs and benefits, they may see the program and assess its performance from several perspectives. The community jobs program, for example, affects the *individuals* who train for the jobs. There are costs and benefits associated with every individual who enrolls in the program, and these figures can be the basis for assessing the program's performance. The training program also affects the *organizations* that hire people. It affects the various levels of *government* that support and that cannot draw taxes from the people who are unemployed. All these groups have different costs, benefits, and agendas for deciding about the relative value of that program.

In a situation like this, it can be difficult to determine the benefits of a program. Does the evaluator use the perspective of the individuals, the organizations who hire them, or the government? Each "level" has different costs, different benefits, and a different perspective. It may not be easy for the evaluator to decide which story to use in the program's analysis.

129

Several years ago, some states began to move mental patients over sixty-five into local nursing homes. The official explanation for these transfers was that the nursing homes provided a "more humane" environment for the older mental patients. It was a tribute to these state officials that they could make this statement with a straight face. The primary reason for those transfers had little to do with a human environment. The moves provided the states with the opportunity to switch the costs for the care of older mental patients from the state mental hospital systems to the federal government through the Medicaid program.

From the states' cost-benefit perspective, the changes were a terrific idea. While the transfers added to the federal government's Medicaid costs, the federal government does not usually conduct cost-benefit analyses. The various long-term care facilities in these states had a rush of new customers. Many of these organizations were undoubtedly happy about the situation. Their cost-benefit indices, if they had them, improved. But for the individuals involved, the results were not so positive.

Many of those new nursing home residents had severe mental disorders. These disorders exacted and continue to exact a cost on the quality of the lives of the other residents. No one apparently thought to measure that diminished benefit. The benefits to the federal government were minimal, if any existed at all. The federal government ended up with a larger Medicaid bill and no benefits to speak of.

When evaluators consider such contrasting perspectives, the central question is, "What is the most sensible thing to do?" The transfer of people did save the individual states a sizable amount of money, but the cost of caring for people in a nursing home is often higher than costs in a state mental institution. Overall, it may have been cheaper and less trouble for everyone concerned to keep those people where they were.

Contrasting costs and benefit perspectives rarely appear in the same equation. In this situation, the individual states and the private institutions received the economic benefits. The federal government and the other nursing home residents assumed the costs. No one looked to see if the equations balanced. If they had, it seems likely that those mental patients would have stayed where they were.

How any program looks depends on the perspective taken. Narrow perspectives are reasonable, but the inability to consider the "larger picture" can be maddening to the conscientious evaluator. Even if the larger picture does not hang together, an evaluator occasionally wants to make the effort, just for the record. If the evaluator doesn't do it, chances are that no one will.

Ethics

Research ethics may not be a major item on the agenda when evaluators first gather to plan their upcoming projects, but a review of ethical principles should be on that agenda. Evaluations affect people's lives, and although evaluators usually realize this, simple awareness is not enough. A list of guidelines, pending ethical problems, and some potential ways of adjusting to them are needed.

For example, when evaluators plan a project, they may select interviews as the primary technique. After some reflection, they decide that interviews might reveal personally embarrassing details. Since the potential is there, it makes sense to be sure at the beginning that interviewers are aware of the problem, and that they take special care to preserve the privacy of the people involved. Another ethical point involves explaining the research process to all parties affected. Although it is not necessary for evaluators to wear a sign saying "Evaluator," it is inappropriate for them to hide their professional identity. One important planning component, then, is to provide a way to introduce everyone to the evaluator and to the evaluation.

What the evaluator does and says during the project and in the report afterwards may affect how employees think about one another and even how they feel about themselves. Not incidentally, that report also may alter the direction of individual careers. When the scope of these effects is considered, it makes sense for evaluators to take the time to consider the implications of their work.

The program participants should not be neglected during these considerations. Those involved in a social program are often a vulnerable group of people. Even if it turns out that the program is not working or if its cost-benefit index is unfavorable, the program's recipients may be deriving considerable benefits from those activities. At the very least, the program gives them a place to go and something to do. Whatever the evaluator may eventually conclude about a program, the feelings of the participants may be affected. Those feelings, and the potential for hurting them, have to be part of the evaluators' ethical considerations.

The program participants are more than ciphers. Some individual or group defined a need and a social program began. The program attracted participants, maybe by promising them an improvement in the quality of their lives. Then, because of a research process that few participants understand or even care about, "they" are thinking about eliminating the program.

Employees, administrators and program managers, and participants are touched by the evaluators' work. Evaluators know that these people are affected by what they do and need to inject that awareness into the research design.

This sympathy need not and should not produce a drastic modification of the design's quality. Nor should it cause a revision of the evaluation results. The evaluation's objectivity cannot be open to mediation, even when ethical concerns are present.

It should be possible to do an evaluation in a way that is sensitive to people's emotions and concerns without compromising the research quality. A little thought and care can go a long way toward preserving positive feelings and alleviating individual concerns. Sensitivity does not require extra resources; only a little more time.

Although there are no mandatory ethical procedures for evaluation research, various professional organizations as well as the federal government publish guidelines for certain research situations. When the research involves human subjects, as most evaluation projects do, those rules can be quite explicit.

The federal government insists that the subjects have a fundamental right to know what the research is about. Few evaluators would argue with that. Federal rules also mandate that participants suffer no discomfort or adverse consequences because of their participation in the research. Here the rules get a little fuzzy.

Program participants could suffer some bad consequences if a program is discontinued. Yet these people are not participants in a research project, not in the strictest sense of that term. There are no indications that court actions have been filed to complain about "adverse consequences" from program evaluations. But in today's litigious world, it may not be long. Although they have no professional choice except to do their jobs, evaluators should be aware of the legal ramifications of what they are doing.

Those federal research guidelines also insist on confidentiality of sensitive information. Few evaluators would disagree with this. Protection of information sources is almost always a fundamental guideline for any research activity, and this includes program evaluation.

During the data-gathering process, evaluators may give express or implied assurances of confidentiality to respondents. People will tell evaluators things, but they often insist, "Don't tell anyone I told you this."

Evaluators have to respect these confidences. Although there is some debate about this point, most researchers feel that promises of confidentiality given to respondents outweigh considerations of completeness or honesty in the report. In other words, if an interviewee tells an evaluator about an incident "in the strictest confidence," the evaluator has to respect that promise. This means that the information given should not appear in the report *unless* the information emerges from another source. Respect of confidentiality is as close to an absolute ethic as it is possible to find in evaluation research.

Other ethical guidelines for evaluators come from professional rather than governmental sources. The concepts of honesty and objectivity in gathering information are ethical as well as methodological canons. The slightest indication that an evaluator has not been completely objective is an ethical lapse every bit as damaging as a methodological one. The evaluator would find out that it is difficult to recover professionally from a substantiated charge of bias.

A lapse in honesty by an evaluator might be harder to find, but it is equally serious. Since dishonesty can be difficult to document, the evaluator's personal ethics are crucial. The evaluator must, within the confines of confidentiality, use information completely and accurately. Any manipulation of the information, well-intentioned though it may be, is professional suicide.

Professional publications provide guidelines for evaluators, but these are often vague or contradictory. They give the researcher little more than a basic sense of what ought to be done in a given situation. Sometimes this is not much help. Several years ago, a researcher doing an evaluation on a social program uncovered systematic stealing by several employees. The individual amounts were not large, only a few dollars, but over time, the cumulative dollar amounts were significant. Unfortunately the only way the evaluator could have discovered this information was from the employees themselves. The individuals who provided the information extracted a promise from the evaluator that the information would be strictly confidential.

"What should I do?" the evaluator wondered. "If I put this information in my report, it violates my pledge to the employees. But if I leave the information out, it is a violation of my professional contract with the organization to provide the most accurate evaluation. And personally, I can't tolerate that kind of dishonesty. I want to see these people punished."

Confidentiality or honesty—it is not an easy choice. Out in the research trenches, it is often not easy to apply the ethical canons of "objectivity," "honesty," and "respect for human subjects" because the application of these principles may be difficult, inappropriate, or conflict with yet another principle. What evaluators "should do" in a given situation may conflict with what they *can* do.

The final decision in many situations involving ethics frequently depends on the character of an individual researcher. It boils down to exactly what the evaluator decides. In cases when one ethic — confidentiality, for example — confronts another, the decision seldom is covered by published guidelines. Resolving the dilemma becomes a personal decision. The evaluator has to weigh the relative merits and decide on the most appropriate course of action.

In difficult situations, perhaps the most fundamental ethical guideline is to think carefully about the implications of each potential action. Evaluators are responsible for whatever actions they take. Since they must stand behind each decision, both professionally and personally, the principal ethical guideline should be: If you think you may regret this action now or five years from now, don't do it! This is as definitive an ethical guideline as evaluators are likely to find.

Response to the Report

Is anyone going to read the report? Probably! But it is also possible that no one will read it. And nothing may happen even if everyone reads that report. It can be unsettling to evaluators when a carefully prepared report sits unread on someone's desk, and even more disconcerting when people read it and do not go out in a mad rush to implement the report's suggestions. Both things happen.

It might be that there wasn't much interest in the evaluation from the beginning. Someone asked for an evaluation because he had to. He had no intention of using the report as a managerial tool. In these cases, no matter what an evaluator did, the report would go to the shelf, unread and unappreciated.

On the other hand, although there may have been some initial interest in having an evaluation, when the report arrived, it may not have been what people wanted. In this case, the evaluator may have to assume responsibility for the report's premature death. Although evaluators cannot force anyone to read a report, they can increase the chances by submitting a "usable" document. Chapter 6 discussed this important point, but it merits repeating.

Whenever individuals or organizations comment on the shortcomings of evaluation reports, the same criticisms appear. In order of their severity, these criticisms are:

1. *Inappropriate or unnecessarily complicated statistical analyses.*
   An earlier chapter made the point that statistics are a means of communication. Once the data are collected, the job of the evaluator is to use statistics that convey the meaning of the data to

the audience. Statistical complexity can easily turn a final report into gobbledygook. Since readers mention this concern so often, evaluators should take a close look at the kind of analysis they plan to do.

2. *Inflexible data-gathering techniques.* Researchers often put a lot of emphasis on questionnaires. The use of this technique is not necessarily bad, except when it precludes the use of other information sources. When the research design is not sufficiently open-ended, the result is an evaluation that is less comprehensive and consequently less productive than it might have been and a report that the audience finds less appealing.

3. *Too goal-oriented.* Although it is important for evaluators to look at a program's goals, they should not ignore the program's other potential effects. Goal analysis is the beginning of a good evaluation, not the end of it.

4. *Inadequate measurements.* Evaluations cannot be effective unless they are based on sound measurements. On occasion, evaluators face situations that make it impossible to use totally reliable measures. If these situations are unavoidable, evaluators have to make the limitations explicit. If they do not, someone else will, to the detriment of the entire evaluation.

5. *Not readable.* Much has already been said on this point and any more would be nagging. But if evaluators cannot make the analysis and discussions understandable to the readers, the report deserves the inattention it gets.

Readers' criticisms aside, there are other factors that could turn even a first-class evaluation report into a useless stack of paper. Political considerations can play a role in deciding how an organization uses an evaluation. If the evaluator's conclusion does not go along with prevailing community values, for example, or if the suggestions in the report annoy an important someone, the evaluation may be headed for that dusty shelf.

There are many reasons, then, for an evaluation report to go unused. Ultimately, the evaluator's satisfaction should come from personal awareness of a job well done, not from what happens as a result of the report. Whatever its inherent frustrations, and there obviously are many of them, program evaluation is an exciting and creative process. For the curious mind, program evaluation offers unique challenges; it is an opportunity to see how things work, to take a social activity apart piece by piece and see how all those parts fit. It is hard to imagine a more rewarding kind of research, even if no one reads that final report.

And Finally . . .

It is obvious by now that program evaluation is an imperfect process. Even with a carefully planned project that has ample time and money, it is difficult to find perfect measures, to use comprehensive data-gathering techniques, and to have the resources for the best research design.

Still, for all its limitations, a competent evaluation process is the best tool that funding agencies, program managers, and policymakers have at their disposal. Despite inherent complexities, unresolved issues, and potential frustrations, evaluation research can make a real contribution to managers, to organizations, and ultimately to society.

Selected Readings

Beauchamp, T., ed. (1975). *Ethics and Public Policy.* Englewood Cliffs, NJ: Prentice Hall.

A variety of essays that deal with major contemporary social issues and the relationship that social research has to the resolution of these problems. This is a good introductory book on ethical issues.

Boswell, J. S. (1976). *Social and Business Enterprises: An Introduction to Organizational Economics.* London: George Allen & Unwin Ltd.

A surprisingly readable economics text, with a very good chapter on the limitations of cost-benefit analysis.

Cohen, B. P. (1989) *Developing Sociological Knowledge: Theory and Method.* Chicago: Nelson-Hall.

A thorough and readable discussion of how scientific information is obtained. Although the author concentrates on sociology, the principles are general.

Deutscher, I. (1979). "Social Theory, Social Programs, and Program Evaluation: A Metatheoretical Note." *Sociological Quarterly,* 20 (Summer): 309–320.

The author argues that the evaluation of social programs offers researchers a good opportunity to examine social theories.

Frankena, W. K. (1963). *Ethics.* Englewood Cliffs, NJ: Prentice Hall.
A good introductory book on general ethics.

Moore, G. E. (1971). *Ethics.* New York: Oxford University Press.
This classic, first published in 1912, provides a good overview of some major ethical issues, including the test of "right and wrong."

Taubes, G. (1993). *Bad Science: The Short Life and Weird Times of Cold Fusion.* New York: Random House.

This examination of the furor raised by the cold fusion "break-through" provides a less than positive look at the ethics of scientific research.

Thompson, M. F. (1980). *Benefit-cost Analysis for Program Evaluation.* Beverly Hills, CA: Sage.
A good overview of cost-benefit analysis.

U.S. Department of Health and Human Services. (1983). "Protection of Human Subjects." OPRR Reports, Code of Federal Regulations 45 CFR 46. Washington, DC: U.S. Government Printing Office.
It will be no surprise to anyone familiar with government publications that this one is difficult to read. But since it does list the guidelines for organizations applying for federal grants, and since some of those organizations might eventually be asking for program evaluations, it makes sense for evaluators to familiarize themselves with the document.

Index